Elmer's Price Guide to Toys

By Elmer Duellman

© 1995
Elmer Duellman

ISBN#: 0-89538-073-0

Published by: L-W Book Sales
                P.O. Box 69
                Gas City, IN 46933

Please write for our free catalog.

Attention Collectors . . . if you would like to contribute photographs or
information of your collection (possibly for profit), please call L-W Books
(toll free) at 1-800-777-6450 Tuesday thru Friday 9am to 3pm.

Layout and design by Stephanie Lane
Photography by David Dilley and Jim Richards

Table of Contents

Dedication

Thank you to my wife, Bernadette, my children, son-in-law, and daughters-in-law. A very special thank you to Rod Shrimpton for all the help in making this book possible.

Pricing Information

The values in this book should be used only as a guide. These prices will vary from one section of the country to the other. All prices are also affected by the condition as well as the demand of the toy.

Neither the Author nor the Publisher assumes responsibility for any gains or losses that might be incurred as a result of using this guide.

Elmer Duellman : The Man Behind the Toys

Elmer was born and still lives in picturesque Fountain City, Wisconsin, a small city along the Mississippi River.

His passion for toy collecting comes from his childhood. Growing up in a family of eight children, there weren't many toys available for any of them to play with.

When he was nine, he started fixing bicycles, then Cushman scooters and motorcycles. At fifteen, Elmer graduated to buying and selling full-sized cars, 42 of them by age eighteen. All of his life has been centered around his family and automobiles.

In 1962 Elmer married his wife Bernadette. They have six children: Les, Rick, Brad, Melissa, Eric and Amanda.

Elmer owned an automotive salvage yard for 30 years; worked at and/or owned a full-service gasoline station and used car dealership since 1951. He drag raced when he was younger and still owns the 1958 Chevrolet he used. Elmer also drove dirt track stock cars successfully for a few years. Today, besides his hobby of collecting and displaying toys, he works at the gas station and car dealership.

Elmer's home and museum is located on top of Eagle Bluff in Fountain City, Wisconsin, the highest point on the Mississippi River. The spectacular view of the river valley accents his collection and museum. Elmer's museum is open to the public one weekend a month from April to October.

Elmer started collecting toys when he was 22 years old. He would purchase all of the toys at local auctions even though everyone else thought he was crazy. He enjoys and owns all types of toys, from the 1800s to modern day collectibles. In his collection and museum you will find a wide variety of toys, antique cars, classic cars, muscle cars, motorcycles, pedal cars, sleds, wagons, scooters and pedal tractors. The toy variety includes pressed steel, Buddy L, Lehmann, Tootsie Toys, Japanese tin, cast iron, and modern day plastic. Elmer particularly enjoys automotive toys, race cars and motorcycles. A couple of the rarest pieces he owns are the Guntherman Gordon Bennett Racer and the Lehmann Boxer Toy.

The most interesting part of owning toys for Elmer is that the toy market is always changing. The prices reflect what people like and enjoy the most. Elmer has fun dealing with people from all over the world. The toy world is VERY large. Elmer thinks toy collecting is something everyone can participate in. You can buy expensive or inexpensive toys and have lots of fun with it.

Elmer likes to share his collection and hopes you enjoy this book. He looks forward to publishing more books of his vast collection.

Look, read and enjoy . . . . .

Miscellaneous Automobiles

Three tone Coupe wind-up, 14½",
by Girard. Made in USA.

Good	Excellent	Mint
$200	$300	$400

Yellow Coupe, 9", made in USA.

Good	Excellent	Mint
$90	$110	$160

Flivver Model T Coupe, 11¼" long, by Buddy L.
Made in USA.

Good	Excellent	Mint
$650	$1000	$1700

Hillclimber, 9".

Good	Excellent	Mint
$90	$175	$280

Miscellaneous Automobiles

1965 Mustang, red, 15¾".
Made in USA.

Good	Excellent	Mint
$65	**$90**	**$130**

1967 Mustang, blue, 15¾".
By Wen Mac, made in USA.

Good	Excellent	Mint
$65	**$100**	**$140**

Turner Packard, 26".

Good	Excellent	Mint
$500	**$1500**	**$2000**

Miscellaneous Automobiles

American National
Roadster, 29".

Good	Excellent	Mint
$3000	$10,000	$15,000

M.G. Sports Car with original box,
9" long. By Hubley, made in USA.

Good	Excellent	Mint
$70	$90	$125

Ice Cream Truck 10¢, plastic, 5¾".

Good	Excellent	Mint
$40	S70	$85

Miscellaneous Automobiles

Plastic Santa in Car, car is
marked "Hi Kids-", 5¹/₂".

Good	Excellent	Mint
$40	**$70**	**$90**

1957 Happy Bunny Car, 5¹/₄".
By Y, Japan.

Good	Excellent	Mint
$100	**$140**	**$175**

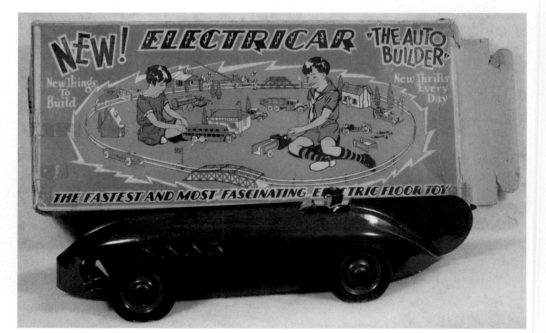

Electricar "The Auto Builder"
with original box, 14¹/₂" long.

Good	Excellent	Mint
$125	**$200**	**$300**

1939 Chevrolet, advertising Roi-Tan Cigars,
4" x 4¹/₂". Made in USA.

Good	Excellent	Mint
$155	**$190**	**$250**

Cast Iron Automobiles

Airflow, 4½".

Good	Excellent	Mint
$160	**$200**	**$250**

Austin, 3¾".

Good	Excellent	Mint
$70	**$85**	**$100**

1929 Chevrolet Arcade, 8¼".

Good	Excellent	Mint
$700	**$1200**	**$1800**

Coupe Champion, 7½".

Good	Excellent	Mint
$225	**$350**	**$400**

Cast Iron Automobiles

Coupe, 3³/₄", die cast.

Good	Excellent	Mint
$75	**$100**	**$125**

Roadster, 4¹/₂".

Good	Excellent	Mint
$125	**$175**	**$200**

Packard Roadster, 26".
By Turner, made in USA.

Good	Excellent	Mint
$300	**$750**	**$1000**

6" long.

Good	Excellent	Mint
$140	**$200**	**$250**

6" long.

Good	Excellent	Mint
$100	**$200**	**$300**

Cast Iron Automobiles

6¹/₂" long.

Good	Excellent	Mint
$250	$400	$500

5" long.

Good	Excellent	Mint
$150	$175	$225

6¹/₂" long.

Good	Excellent	Mint
$150	$200	$240

6¹/₂" long.

Good	Excellent	Mint
$300	$500	$750

4" long.

Good	Excellent	Mint
$125	$175	$200

5³/₄ ' long.

Good	Excellent	Mint
$110	$180	$250

Cast Iron Automobiles

4½" long.

Good	Excellent	Mint
$90	**$120**	**$160**

Barclay Build and Paint Your Own Auto Set, with original box, 5½" x 4½". Made in North Bergen N.J.

Good	Excellent	Mint
$125	**$170**	**$225**

1930's Cor Cor Grahm, 20" long, pressed steel. Made in USA.

Good	Excellent	Mint
$750	**$1300**	**$1800**

Andy Gump, 7", by Arcade.

Good	Excellent
$1500	**$3200**

Andy Gump, 2¾", by Tootsie Toy.

Good	Excellent	Mint
$140	**$200**	**$375**

Imported Automobiles

Aston-Martin (James Bond Car) as seen in the movies "Goldfinger" and "Thunderball" with original box. Battery powered automatic action, 11", by Gilbert.

Good	Excellent	Mint
$100	$225	$300

M101 Aston-Martin Secret Ejector Car, (James Bond) remote control with original box, 11½". By A.C. Gilbert Co., made in Japan.

Good	Excellent	Mint
$150	$220	$275

1960's Austin Healey, 8". By Bandai, Japan.

Good	Excellent	Mint
$55	$95	$135

Imported Automobiles

BMW 1500, 8½", with original box.

Good	Excellent	Mint
$150	**$225**	**$300**

BMW 2000 CS, battery operated remote control, in original box, 8". By Bandai, Japan.

Good	Excellent	Mint
$100	**$165**	**$190**

BMW 2000-CS, battery operated with bump and go action, roaring engine, blinking blue and red lights in the rear seat, all metal, with original box, 11". By Yonezewa, Japan.

Good	Excellent	Mint
$600	**$800**	**$1000**

Imported Automobiles

Citroen, 8", by Bandai, Japan.

Good	Excellent	Mint
$65	$115	$150

Ferrari Superamerica Coupe with original box, 11" long. By Bandai, Japan.

Good	Excellent	Mint
$165	$290	$400

Ferrari with gear shift, battery operated, from Sears, with original box, 11" long. By Bandai, Japan

Good	Excellent	Mint
$65	$100	$185

Imported Automobiles

Fiat 600, 7", by Bandai, Japan.

Good	Excellent	Mint
$50	**$85**	**$120**

Isetta 588, friction car with original box, 6½". By Bandai, Japan.

Good	Excellent	Mint
$90	**$150**	**$200**

Jaguar, 6", made in Japan.

Good	Excellent	Mint
$80	**$120**	**$175**

Jaguar Sedan, 8¼", by Bandai, Japan.

Good	Excellent	Mint
$90	**$125**	**$150**

Imported Automobiles

XKE Jaguar, 8¼", by Haji, Japan.

Good	Excellent	Mint
$95	$180	$220

Jaguar E-Type, friction powered, with original box, 11". By TN, Japan.

Good	Excellent	Mint
$250	$320	$380

Late 1950's M.G.A. 1600 Coupe, 8", with original box, friction powered. By Bandai, Japan.

Good	Excellent	Mint
$75	$110	$165

Imported Automobiles

M.G. Convertible, friction powered, 10½", made in Japan.

Good	Excellent	Mint
$800	**$1100**	**$1400**

M.G. Convertible Roadster, 7", by Bandai Japan.

Good	Excellent	Mint
$80	**$120**	**$160**

Mercedes, battery powered, 10", by Alps, Japan.

Good	Excellent	Mint
$200	**$250**	**$300**

14

Imported Automobiles

Mercedes MB250 SE, friction powered, 7".
Made in Japan.

Good	Excellent	Mint
$30	$50	$75

Mercedes, 7", made in Japan.

Good	Excellent	Mint
$50	$90	$120

Mercedes 250 S.E., friction powered, 7¼",
with original box, made in Japan.

Good	Excellent	Mint
$45	$60	$75

Opel, friction powered, 11½", made in Japan.

Good	Excellent	Mint
$200	$300	$400

Imported Automobiles

1960's Opel Rekord Sedan, with original box, 10¾", by Bandai, Japan.

Good	Excellent	Mint
$100	**$175**	**$225**

Porsche Electro Majic 7500 Convertible, 10", battery powered, with original box. By Distler, Japan.

Good	Excellent	Mint
$500	**$690**	**$780**

Porsche (World News), 9¾", made in Japan.

Good	Excellent	Mint
$200	**$290**	**$350**

Imported Automobiles

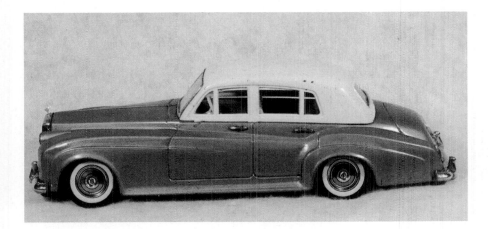

Rolls-Royce, 11", by Bandai,
Japan.

Good	Excellent	Mint
$160	**$300**	**$485**

1960's Rolls-Royce Silver Cloud
Sedan, 11¾", with original box.
By Bandai, Japan.

Good	Excellent	Mint
$160	**$300**	**$485**

Rolls-Royce Silver Cloud Sedan, 12",
with original box. By Bandai, Japan.

Good	Excellent	Mint
$160	**$300**	**$485**

Imported Automobiles

Mercedes, 8³/₄", by Schuco, Germany.

Good	Excellent	Mint
$165	**$210**	**$240**

Porsche Electro Majic 7500, 10", with original box. By Distler, Germany.

Good	Excellent	Mint
$500	**$690**	**$780**

Porsche Electro Majic 7500, 10", with original box. By Distler, Germany.

Good	Excellent	Mint
$500	**$690**	**$780**

Imported Automobiles

Porsche wind-up, 8½", by Gescha, Germany.

Good	Excellent	Mint
$225	**$300**	**$385**

B.M.W. Convertibles, three different colors, 10", by Distler.

Good	Excellent	Mint
$150	**$275**	**$325**

Citroen 4 Dr., friction powered, 8".

Good	Excellent	Mint
$150	**$200**	**$300**

Imported Automobiles

1956 Isetta, 4".

Good	Excellent	Mint
$150	**$220**	**$280**

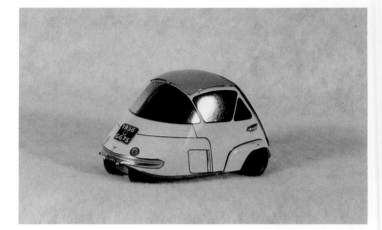

Porsche Electro Majic 7500, 10",
by Distler.

Good	Excellent	Mint
$500	**$690**	**$780**

Rolls-Royce Custom Convertible,
10¾". By Lennie, made in USA.

$300

Kingsbury Automobiles

Kingsbury Sedan, 13",
made in USA.

Good	Excellent	Mint
$1500	**$2000**	**$2800**

Kingsbury Sedan, 12½",
made in USA.

Good	Excellent	Mint
$350	**$400**	**$700**

Airflow, wind-up with
electric lights, 14½".
By Kingsbury, USA.

Good	Excellent	Mint
$300	**$450**	**$650**

Kingsbury Automobiles

Musical Coupe, wind-up, with
battery operated lights, 12¾".
By Kingsbury, USA.

Good	Excellent	Mint
$1200	$1600	$1890

Huckster, 14½", by Kingsbury,
USA.

Good	Excellent	Mint
$1500	$2000	$3000

Roadster, 12", by Kingsbury, USA.

Good	Excellent	Mint
$500	$900	$1200

Tin Automobiles

Saloon Car, wind-up, 9",
with original box.
Made in England.

Good	Excellent	Mint
$90	$125	$190

Chrysler Airflow, 4¾", made in
France.

Good	Excellent	Mint
$70	$100	$125

Fischer Touring Car, 11".
Made in Germany.

Good	Excellent	Mint
$800	$1100	$1400

Tin Automobiles

Hessmobile, wind-up, 9".
Made in Germany.

Good	Excellent	Mint
$600	**$900**	**$1200**

Horseless Carriage, wind-up, 4½".
By Bine, Germany.

Good	Excellent	Mint
$475	**$800**	**$1000**

Limousine, 8¾", by Garrette, Germany.

Good	Excellent
$3000	**$4800**

Model T Coupe, 6¾", by Bing, Germany.

Good	Excellent	Mint
$300	**$490**	**$700**

Tin Automobiles

Wind-up car, 10½". Made in Germany.

Good   Excellent   Mint
$800 $1100 $1300

Wind-up Car with battery operated lights. By Distler, Germany.

Good   Excellent   Mint
$1650 $2000 $2600

Wind-up, 6", made in Germany.

Good   Excellent   Mint
$250 $300 $400

Tin Automobiles

German wind-up car, 7¾".

Good	Excellent	Mint
$120	**$190**	**$250**

Sedan with opening rear doors, 5¾". By Orobr, Germany.

Good	Excellent	Mint
$200	**$390**	**$475**

Sedan wind-up, 11", made in Germany.

Good	Excellent	Mint
$900	**$1200**	**$1450**

Tin Automobiles

Sedan, 4 cycle piston, 8¹⁴".
By Kohnstam, Germany.

Good	Excellent	Mint
$650	**$850**	**$1000**

Sedan wind-up, 10½".
By Tipp, Germany.

Good	Excellent	Mint
$500	**$750**	**$900**

Toyville Express, 8½", by Honpareil.

Good	Excellent	Mint
$150	**$270**	**$375**

Tin Automobiles

Prewar Chrysler Airflows, 3½".
Made in Japan.

Set with box – **$390**
or each individual – **$65**

Graham Paige, 5½", with
original box. By
CK, Japan.

Good	Excellent	Mint
$130	**$180**	**$230**

Star Car, 9¾", prewar.
Made in Japan.

Good	Excellent	Mint
$1100	**$1750**	**$2300**

Tin Automobiles

"Old Jalopy", 7", by Marx.

Good	Excellent	Mint
$100	**$150**	**$175**

Trikauto wind-up, with original box, 8". By Strauss, made in USA.

Good	Excellent	Mint
$400	**$700**	**$890**

1918 Wind-up Auto, 7³/₄", made by N.Y.

Good	Excellent	Mint
$130	**$190**	**$250**

Two old cars: Left – 8¹/₄": Right – 8³/₄", by Marx. Made in USA.

Good	Excellent	Mint
$200	**$375**	**$475**

Tin Automobiles

Avanti, friction powered,
8¼". By Bandai, Japan.

Good   Excellent   Mint
$110   **$125**   **$275**

Studebaker Avanti, 8½".
By Bandai, Japan.

Good   Excellent   Mint
$170   **$225**   **$275**

1960 Buick 4 door, friction
powered. By ICHIKO,
Japan.

Good   Excellent   Mint
$450   **$690**   **$900**

1961 Buick 4 door, friction
powered, 15½". Made in
Japan.

Good   Excellent   Mint
$350   **$500**   **$650**

Tin Automobiles

Buick Riviera, 10¾".
By Haji, Japan.

Good   Excellent   Mint
$250   **$400**   **$500**

1933 Cadillac, 8¼".
By Bandai, Japan.

Good   Excellent   Mint
$25   **$60**   **$90**

1933 Cadillac, 8¼".
By Bandai, Japan.

Good   Excellent   Mint
$25   **$60**   **$90**

1959 Cadillac, 12½".
By Bandai, Japan.

Good   Excellent   Mint
$100   **$200**   **$300**

Tin Automobiles

1959 Cadillac, 11½", by Bandai, Japan.

Good	Excellent	Mint
$100	**$200**	**$300**

1960 Cadillac, friction powered, 18". By Y, Japan.

Good	Excellent	Mint
$390	**$650**	**$800**

1960 Cadillac, 18", by Yonezawa, Japan.

Good	Excellent	Mint
$390	**$650**	**$800**

Tin Automobiles

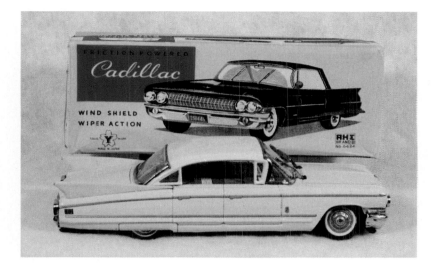

1960 Cadillac, friction powered, 9", by Y, Japan.

Good	Excellent	Mint
$160	**$200**	**$240**

1961 Cadillac, battery operated, 16¾", by Bandai, Japan.

Good	Excellent	Mint
$290	**$475**	**$600**

1961 Cadillac, battery operated, 16¾", by SSS, Japan.

Good	Excellent	Mint
$350	**$600**	**$700**

Tin Automobiles

1961 Cadillac, 9", made in Japan.

Good   Excellent   Mint
$80   **$140**   **$195**

Cadillac Convertible, 8", made in Japan.

Good   Excellent   Mint
$100   **$150**   **$185**

Cadillac, 9½", made in Japan.

Good   Excellent   Mint
$60   **$90**   **$135**

Cadillac, 12", by Gama, Germany.

Good   Excellent   Mint
$400   **$650**   **$875**

Tin Automobiles

Cadillac Convertible, battery operated, 10½", made in Japan.

Good	Excellent	Mint
$65	$90	$150

Cadillac with working headlights, 12¾". By Marusan, Japan.

Good	Excellent	Mint
$750	$1175	$1400

Cadillac with working headlights, 12¾". By Marusan, Japan.

Good	Excellent	Mint
$750	$1175	$1400

Tin Automobiles

Cadillac Convertible, friction powered, 11¼". By Alps, Japan.

Good	Excellent	Mint
$600	**$1100**	**$1500**

Cadillac Convertible, 13½". By Nomura, Japan.

Good	Excellent	Mint
$200	**$350**	**$500**

Cadillac, with original box, 12¼". By Marusan, Japan.

Good	Excellent	Mint
$450	**$700**	**$900**

Tin Automobiles

Cadillac, 12". By
Gama, Germany.

Good | Excellent | Mint
$400 | $650 | $875

Cadillac, friction powered,
with original box, 11½".
By Bandai, Japan.

Good | Excellent | Mint
$90 | $200 | $300

1960's Cadillac Sedan,
with original box, 13".
By Bandai, Japan.

Good | Excellent | Mint
$80 | $200 | $350

Tin Automobiles

1950's Remote Control
Cragstan Cadillac, with
original box, 9".
By Macoma, Japan.

Good	Excellent	Mint
$35	**$70**	**$95**

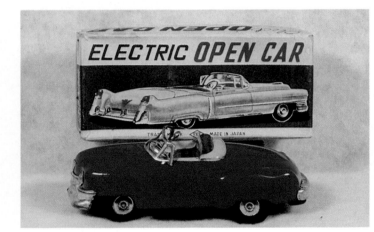

Cadillac, Electric Open Car,
with original box, 7".
By KKK, Japan.

Good	Excellent	Mint
$75	**$100**	**$125**

Cadillac Convertible, 11½".
By Alps, Japan.

Good	Excellent	Mint
$600	**$1100**	**$1500**

Tin Automobiles

Cadillac Fleetwood
Eldorado Ride-On Friction,
28", with original box.
By Ichiko, Japan.

Good   Excellent   Mint
$450   **$650**   **$800**

1967 Camaro, yellow with
black top, 11¼".
Made in Japan.

Good   Excellent   Mint
$100   **$200**   **$300**

1967 Camaro, battery
operated with clear hood so
you can view the engine,
13". Made in Japan.

Good   Excellent   Mint
$100   **$140**   **$220**

Tin Automobiles

1967 Camaro, battery operated, red with black top, 11". Made in Japan.

Good	Excellent	Mint
$100	**$200**	**$300**

1962 Chevy Custom, by Lennie, made in USA.

Mint
$600

1954 Chevy, grey with black top, 11". By Line Mac Toys.

Good	Excellent	Mint
$800	**$1100**	**$1300**

Tin Automobiles

1955 Chevrolet, 9¼" long.
By Ichiko, Japan.

Good	Excellent	Mint
$75	$180	$260

1955 Chevrolet, 9¼" long. By Ichiko, Japan.

Good	Excellent	Mint
$90	$200	$325

1959 Chevrolet, friction powered, 10" long. By ASC, Japan.

Good	Excellent	Mint
$90	$140	$220

1959 Chevrolet Convertible, friction powered, 7¼"
long. Made in Japan.

Good	Excellent	Mint
$60	$90	$110

1961 Chevy Impala, friction powered, battery opperated lights,
11", made in Japan.

Good	Excellent	Mint
$200	$425	$500

Tin Automobiles

1961 Chevy Impala Sport
Sedan, red four door, with
original box, 11", by
Bandai, Japan.

Good	Excellent	Mint
$225	**$300**	**$450**

1961 Chevy Impala Sport
Sedan, white four door, with
original box, 11", by Bandai,
Japan.

Good	Excellent	Mint
$225	**$300**	**$450**

1963 Chevy Convertible, friction powered, 8". By Haji, Japan.

Good	Excellent	Mint
$125	**$175**	**$225**

1963 Chevy, opening doors, 8¼". By Haji, Japan.

Good	Excellent	Mint
$150	**$200**	**$250**

Tin Automobiles

1963 Chevy black four door, 13¼".
Made in Japan.

Good	Excellent	Mint
$300	**$500**	**$650**

1960 Corvair, 5½", made in Japan.

Good	Excellent	Mint
$35	**$65**	**$85**

Corvair Convertible, friction
powered, with original box,
9". By Cragston, Japan.

Good	Excellent	Mint
$140	**$220**	**$300**

Two Corvairs, red and blue,
8¼", by Bandai, Japan.

Good	Excellent	Mint
$80	**$110**	**$150**

Tin Automobiles

Corvette, blue with white top, friction powered, 8¼", by Bandai, Japan.

Good	Excellent	Mint
$75	**$100**	**$150**

Corvette Sting Ray Sport Coupe, with original box, powered by battery driven motor. By Ichida, Japan.

Good	Excellent	Mint
$350	**$450**	**$600**

Chrysler Convertible, 9½", by Yonezawa, Japan.

Good	Excellent	Mint
$300	**$400**	**$490**

Tin Automobiles

Chrysler Convertible, grey, 9¾", with original box. By Yonezawa, Japan.

Good	Excellent	Mint
$300	$400	$490

Chrysler Imperial Crown Sedan, yellow with white top, with original box, 8½". By Bandai, Japan.

Good	Excellent	Mint
$85	$125	$165

Chrysler Imperial, white with a red top, 8¼". By Bandai, Japan.

Good	Excellent	Mint
$85	$125	$165

1958 Edsel, white and red, with a grey top, 11", by ATC, Japan.

Good	Excellent	Mint
$500	$600	$675

Tin Automobiles

Falcon, red with black top & four
door, 8", made in Japan.

Good	Excellent	Mint
$50	**$80**	**$100**

1963 Falcon, turquoise four
door, 8". By Bandai, Japan.

Good	Excellent	Mint
$50	**$70**	**$85**

Maverick, green, 7½", made
in Japan.

Good	Excellent	Mint
$60	**$100**	**$125**

Model A's with original box,
6¼" each. By Bandai, Japan.

Set with box – **$325**

Tin Automobiles

1965 Mustang, friction powered, 15½". By TN, Japan.

Good	Excellent	Mint
$180	**$250**	**$300**

1965 Mustang Convertible, with original box, 4⅛". By Tekno, Denmark.

Good	Excellent	Mint
$40	**$70**	**$90**

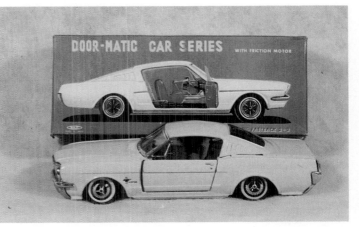

1965 Mustang Fastback, with original box, marked "Door-Matic Car Series" with friction motor, 8". By Haji, Japan.

Good	Excellent	Mint
$130	**$190**	**$250**

1965 Mustang, yellow with black top, 10½", by Bandai, Japan.

Good	Excellent	Mint
$120	**$185**	**$225**

1969 Mustang, battery operated, 10", by Taiyo, Japan.

Good	Excellent	Mint
$45	**$85**	**$110**

Tin Automobiles

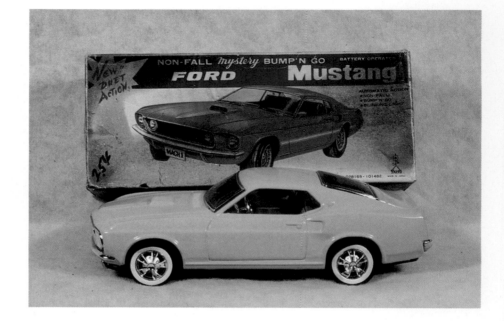

Mustang, bump'n go, battery operated, with original box, 9½". By Taiyo, Japan.

Good	Excellent	Mint
$60	**$80**	**$120**

Thunderbird Speedster Convertible, 7", made in Japan.

Good	Excellent	Mint
$80	**$110**	**$140**

Thunderbird Speedster Convertible, 10½", battery operated with original box. By TN, Japan.

Good	Excellent	Mint
$150	**$350**	**$500**

Tin Automobiles

Thunderbird, with original box, marked "Marvellous Car". Battery operated, 11", by TN, Japan.

Good	Excellent	Mint
$200	**$245**	**$325**

Ford Thunderbird Sedan, with original box, friction powered, 8¼". By Bandai, Japan.

Good	Excellent	Mint
$100	**$140**	**$180**

Thunderbird, 8". By Bandai, Japan.

Good	Excellent	Mint
$80	**$120**	**$140**

1963 Thunderbird, red with white top, with original box, marked "Door-Matic Car Series" with friction motor, 8½". By Bandai, Japan.

Good	Excellent	Mint
$140	**$180**	**$225**

Tin Automobiles

Thunderbird, friction powered, 11", by Bandai, Japan.

Good	Excellent	Mint
$120	**$190**	**$250**

Ford Thunderbird Convertible, with original box, 12", friction powered. By ATC, Japan.

Good	Excellent	Mint
$150	**$250**	**$350**

Thunderbird Convertible, retractable wind-up, friction powered, 15½". Made in Japan.

Good	Excellent	Mint
$150	**$210**	**$290**

Tin Automobiles

Ford Thunderbird Convertible, door-matic action, with original box, 8". By Haji, Japan.

Good	Excellent	Mint
$160	$200	$250

Thunderbird Convertible, door-matic action, with original box, friction powered, 8". By Haji, Japan.

Good	Excellent	Mint
$160	$200	$250

Ford Thunderbird Convertible, with original box, friction powered, 8". By Bandai, Japan.

Good	Excellent	Mint
$110	$160	S195

Thunderbird Convertible, with sliding roof, friction powered, 8". By Bandai, Japan.

Good	Excellent	Mint
$85	$120	$145

Tin Automobiles

Ford Thunderbird Convertible,
with original box, 8", friction
powered. By Bandai, Japan.

Good	Excellent	Mint
$100	**$140**	**$175**

Thunderbird, battery operated,
remote control, 10½". Made in
Japan.

Good	Excellent	Mint
$150	**$210**	**$280**

1952 Ford, two door, 8" long.
Made in Japan.

Good	Excellent	Mint
$150	**$250**	**$300**

1955 Ford, two door convertible,
friction powered, 7½" long, with
original box. By Haji, Japan.

Good	Excellent	Mint
$100	**$170**	**$230**

Tin Automobiles

1956 Ford, battery operated,
8¾" long. By Asahi Toy, Japan.

Good Excellent Mint
$60 $110 $145

1956 Ford Convertible,
7½" long. By Irco, Japan.

Good Excellent Mint
$160 $225 $300

1956 Ford Convertible, 11½" long.
By Haji, Japan.

Good Excellent Mint
$2300 $3200 $4500

Tin Automobiles

1956 Ford, 8" long.
Made in Japan.

Good	Excellent	Mint
$200	**$300**	**$390**

1957 Ford, friction powered,
9¾" long. By ATC, Japan.

Good	Excellent	Mint
$250	**$300**	**$350**

1957 Ford, friction powered,
9¾". By ATC, Japan.

Good	Excellent	Mint
$250	**$300**	**$350**

1957 Ford Convertible, friction
powered, 7¼". By Haji, Japan.

Good	Excellent	Mint
$120	**$200**	**$240**

Tin Automobiles

1957 Ford, friction powered,
8¼". Made in Japan.

Good	Excellent	Mint
$50	$80	$100

1957 Ford, friction powered
with siren, with original box,
9¼". By Ichico, Japan.

Good	Excellent	Mint
$250	$300	$350

1957 Ford Convertible,
11½". By Bandai, Japan.

Good	Excellent	Mirt
$260	$385	$580

Tin Automobiles

1958 Ford Skyliner Sports Car, battery operated with retractable top, 9". By TN, Japan.

Good	Excellent	Mint
$120	**$180**	**$225**

1958 Ford with retractable top, friction powered, 10¾". Made in Japan.

Good	Excellent	Mint
$120	**$220**	**$250**

1959 Ford two door Sedan, 8", made in Japan.

Good	Excellent	Mint
$80	**$110**	**$145**

1959 Ford Convertible, 8", made in Japan.

Good	Excellent	Mint
$55	**$90**	**$150**

Tin Automobiles

1960 Ford Sedan two door, friction motor, 11½". Made in Japan.

Good	Excellent	Mint
$80	$120	$190

1962 Ford, Airport Serice Car, friction powered, 9½". By TT, Japan.

Good	Excellent	Mint
$70	$100	$140

1962 Ford, friction powered, 9½". By TT, Japan.

Good	Excellent	Mint
$45	$65	$90

1963 Ford, Coca Cola, friction powered, 10¾", by Taiyo, Japan.

Good	Excellent	Mint
$150	$250	$320

Tin Automobiles

1963 Ford, 7-Up,
friction powered, 10³/₄".
By Taiyo, Japan.

Good	Excellent	Mint
$140	**$200**	**$280**

1963 Ford, Pepsi Cola,
friction powered, 10³/₄",
by Taiyo, Japan.

Good	Excellent	Mint
$140	**$200**	**$280**

1960 Ford two door, 7¹/₂".
Made in Japan.

Good	Excellent	Mint
$60	**$100**	**$160**

Tin Automobiles

Ford two door, 7½", by T.N., Japan.

Good	Excellent	Mint
$60	$85	$110

Ford, United Air Lines, 8¾", by ASC Japan.

Good	Excellent	Mint
$90	$120	$140

1955 Lincoln, blue with white top, four door, 12½", made in Japan.

Good	Excellent	Mint
$900	$1200	$1500

1958 Lincoln, red with black top, two door, 11½". By Bandai, Japan.

Good	Excellent	Mint
$100	$190	$285

Tin Automobiles

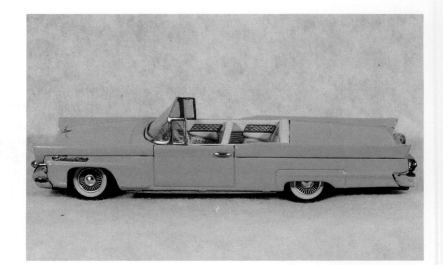

1958 Lincoln Convertible,
11½", by Bandai, Japan.

Good	Excellent	Mint
$140	**$240**	**$325**

Continental Super Special,
friction powered motor, 13½",
with original box. By Cragstan,
West Germany.

Good	Excellent	Mint
$100	**$150**	**$200**

Lincoln Convertible,
friction powered, 11¾".
Made in Japan.

Good	Excellent	Mint
$140	**$240**	**$325**

Tin Automobiles

Lincoln, 7¼", by Yonezawa, Japan.

Good	Excellent	Mint
$225	$300	$480

1953 Mercury, with original box, battery operated, 9½". By Rock Valley Toy, Japan.

Good	Excellent	Mint
$160	$225	$275

Oldsmobile Toronado, 15½", by ATC, Japan.

Good	Excellent	Mint
$225	$300	$390

Tin Automobiles

1958 Oldsmobile, red with
white top, 13", by Yonezawa,
Japan.

Good	Excellent	Mint
$450	**$600**	**$750**

1959 Oldsmobile, two door,
friction powered, 13", made
in Japan.

Good	Excellent	Mint
$300	**$450**	**$585**

Oldsmobile Toronado,
two door, 15½". By ATC,
Japan.

Good	Excellent	Mint
$225	**$300**	**$390**

Tin Automobiles

1953 Packard Convertible,
16", by Alps, Japan.

Good	Excellent	Mint
$2800	$4000	$5000

1953 Packard, four door,
16½", by Alps, Japan.

Good	Excellent	Mint
$2900	$3500	$4200

1958 Packard Convertible,
10¾", by Schuco, West Germany.

Good	Excellent	Mint
$400	$365	$800

Tin Automobiles

Two Packard's with one
original box, 10¼".
By Distler, Germany.

Good   Excellent   Mint
$200 $325 $400

1954 Pontiac, two door, black, 10",
friction powered. By Asahi Toy, Japan.

Good   Excellent   Mint
$300 $600 $850

1956 Plymouth Mystery Car,
battery operated, automatic
reversing, with original box,
11¾". By Alps, Japan.

Good   Excellent   Mint
$1000 $1400 $1700

Tin Automobiles

1957 Plymouth, friction powered with siren, with original box, 6¼". Made in Japan.

Good	Excellent	Mint
$75	$110	$140

1957 Plymouth, friction powered with siren, with original box, 6¼". Made in Japan.

Good	Excellent	Mint
$75	$110	$140

1959 Plymouth Convertible, friction powered, 8¼". By Bandai, Japan.

Good	Excellent	Mint
$110	$180	$230

1959 Plymouth, 8¼". By Bandai, Japan.

Good	Excellent	Mint
$95	$155	$185

Tin Automobiles

1959 Plymouth, four door, 10³/₄",
by ATC, Japan.

Good	Excellent	Mint
$600	**$850**	**$1000**

1963 Plymouth Valiant Sedan, friction
powered, 8¹/₄", with original box. By
Bandai, Japan.

Good	Excellent	Mint
$50	**$90**	**$120**

1963 Plymouth Valiant Sedan, friction
powered, 8¹/₄", with original box. By
Bandai, Japan.

Good	Excellent	Mint
$50	**$90**	**$120**

1963 Plymouth Valiant Sedan, friction
powered, 8¹/₄", with original box. By
Bandai, Japan.

Good	Excellent	Mint
$50	**$90**	**$120**

Tin Automobiles

1964 Plymouth Fury, friction powered with siren, 10", with original box. By Kusama, Japan.

Good	Excellent	Mint
$100	$170	$200

Plymouth Valiant, four door, blue with white top, 8". Made in Japan.

Good	Excellent	Mint
$40	$80	$100

1961 Rambler Classic Sedan, friction powered, 8', with original box. By Bandai, Japan.

Good	Excellent	Mint
$80	$125	$165

Touring Car, convertible, 10". Made in Japan.

Good	Excellent	Mint
$65	$110	$145

Pan Am Jeep, 5¾", made in Japan.

Good	Excellent	Mint
$30	$50	$75

Tin Automobiles

Town Service Center Jeep, 8",
by Y, Japan.

Good	Excellent	Mint
$60	**$90**	**$125**

Construction Jeep with box, 8",
by Marasan.

set with box – **$250**

Volkswagen, Mystery Action,
battery operated, 9¾", by KO,
Japan.

Good	Excellent	Mint
$100	**$170**	**$200**

Tin Automobiles

Volkswagen, friction powered, 7¹/²",
made in Japan.

Good	Excellent	Mint
$100	$130	$150

Volkswagen, split window,
wind-up, 9", made in Japan.

Good	Excellent	Mint
$320	$450	$585

Volkswagen, 1500 Sedan, 7", with original
box, friction powered. Made in Japan.

Good	Excellent	Mint
$45	$65	$85

Volkswagen 1600TL, friction motor, with
original box. Made in Japan.

Good	Excellent	Mint
$45	$65	$85

Volkswagen 1600 Sedan, friction drive,
with original box, 8". By Bandai, Japan.

Good	Excellent	Mint
$35	$70	$90

Volkswagen, 7¹/²", by TN, Japan.

Good	Excellent	Mint
$100	$140	165

Tin Automobiles

Smoking Volkswagen, battery operated, and stop and go mystery action, 10", with original box. By Aoshin, Japan.

Good	Excellent	Mint
$50	**$90**	**$120**

Liliput Auto's, wind-up, with original boxes, 2⁵⁄₈". By Distler, Germany.

Good	Excellent	Mint
$50	**$70**	**$85**

Tri-ang Minic Toys, with original box, 11" x 11" set, made in England.

Set with box – **Rare $1400**

Tin Automobiles

Cities Service Station, battery operated, 10½", with original box. By Linemar Toys.

Good	Excellent	Mint
$150	**$200**	**$250**

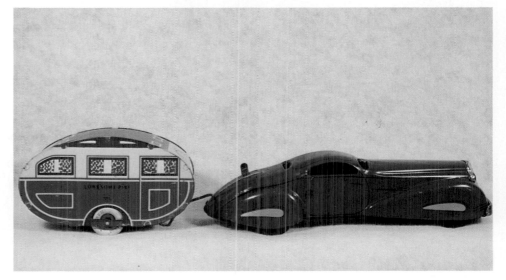

Lonesome Pine Trailer & Coupe, wind-up, 22", by Marx, USA.

Good	Excellent	Mint
$425	**$650**	**$775**

Musical Car, battery operated, 7", by K, Japan.

Good	Excellent	Mint
$120	**$180**	**$250**

Tin Automobiles

Schuco Car, #1010, 5$^{1/2}$",
by Schuco, Germany.

Good	Excellent	Mint
$65	**$100**	**$150**

Electric Skyliner, battery operated,
with original box, 8$^{3/4}$". Made in Japan.

Good	Excellent	Mint
$125	**$220**	**$275**

Fex 1111, SOS, 5$^{3/4}$", with
original box. By Schuco,
Germany.

Good	Excellent	Mint
$75	**$140**	**$175**

Tin Automobiles

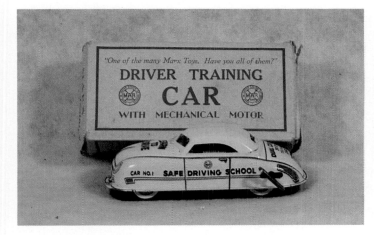

Driver Training Car with mechanical motor, wind-up, 6½", with original box. By Marx, made in USA.

Good	Excellent	Mint
$65	$90	$150

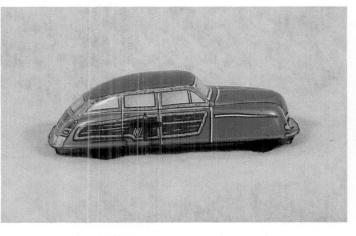

Woody Stationwagon, wind-up, 7½". By Marx, made in USA.

Good	Excellent	Mint
$80	$100	$140

Woody Stationwagon, friction powered, 7". By Courtland Toys, made in USA.

Good	Excellent	Mint
$80	$100	$130

Woody Stationwagon, wind-up, 5".

Good	Excellent	Mint
$80	$100	$140

Hotel New York Airport, 7", by Bandai, Japan.

Good	Excellent	Mint
$80	$120	$160

Little Pig Tin Convertible, 6", made in Japan.

Good	Excellent	Mint
$50	$75	$125

Tin Automobiles

Bumper Car, wind-up, 9¼".

Good	Excellent	Mint
$100	**$170**	**$225**

Mouse in a car with a balloon, 5¾",
by Schuco, Germany.

Good	Excellent	Mint
$130	**$200**	**$240**

Hod Rod Special, battery operated,
9½", made in Japan.

Good	Excellent	Mint
$85	**$150**	**$200**

Just Married car with couple,
10½", with original box.
By Alps, Japan

Good	Excellent	Mint
$120	**$200**	**$250**

Tin Automobiles

1950's Cadillac Convertible, battery operated, stop and go car with light and automatic opening door, 8¼", with original box. By Marusan, Japan.

Good	Excellent	Mint
$80	$110	$165

Convertible with man in car, 7¼", friction powered. Made in Japan.

Good	Excellent	Mint
$60	$90	$120

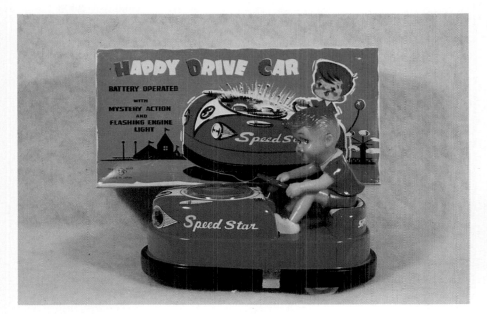

Happy Drive Car, battery operated, with mystery action and flashing engine light, 8" with original box. By T.N., Japan.

Good	Excellent	Mint
$35	$70	$90

Automobiles with Trailers

Car and Trailer, red, 26" long together, by Wyandotte, USA.

Good	Excellent	Mint
$450	**$600**	**$800**

Car and Trailer, blue, 26" long together, by Wyandotte, USA.

Good	Excellent	Mint
$450	**$600**	**$800**

Car and Trailer, green, 25" long together, by Wyandotte, USA.

Good	Excellent	Mint
$250	**$480**	**$700**

Automobiles with Trailers

1950's Car and Trailer's that match,, 7½", made in Japan.

Good	Excellent	Mint
$15	$35	$50

U-Haul Wagon and Trailer, 9", by Lucky Toy, Japan.

Good	Excellent	Mint
$45	$60	$75

Rambler Station Wagon & Shasta Travel Trailer,"Holiday Express", 22½", with original box. By Bandai, Japan.

Good	Excellent	Mint
$350	$440	$575

Automobiles with Trailers

Lincoln & Shasta Travel
Trailer, 22". By Bandai,
Japan.

Good	Excellent	Mint
$400	**$500**	**$650**

Falcon and Trailer, 17", made
in Japan.

Good	Excellent	Mint
$60	**$100**	**$175**

Trailer, friction powered, 9", with
original box. By SSS Toys,
Japan.

Good	Excellent	Mint
$80	**$100**	**$150**

Automobiles with Trailers

This set includes a Rambler Station Wagon, Viking Cabin Cruiser, Trailer, and a Johnson Outboard Motor. Marked on box "The Weekend Skipper II", 22½". By Bandai, Japan.

Good	Excellent	Mint
$190	**$300**	**$375**

A 1960 Cadillac, friction powered, with a boat on a trailer and an outboard motor and water skis, with original box, 21". Made in Japan

Good	Excellent	Mint
$200	**$260**	**$300**

Station Wagons

Buick Wagon, friction powered, 8¼",
by Bandai, Japan.

Good	Excellent	Mint
$100	$135	$165

Buick Wagon, friction powered, 8¼",
by Bandai, Japan.

Good	Excellent	Mint
$100	$135	$165

1959 Buick Station Wagon, friction
powered, 8¾", by Y, Japan.

Good	Excellent	Mint
$85	$120	$150

Buick Station Wagon,
friction powered, 15".
By Asakusa, Japan.

Good	Excellent	Mint
$200	$290	$350

Station Wagons

1954 Buick Century Wagon, with electric headlights, remote control, with original box, 8¹ᐟ²". By Irco, Japan

Good	Excellent	Mint
$100	$140	$175

1960 Chevrolet Wagon, 8³ᐟ⁴", by Alps, Japan.

Good	Excellent	Mint
$45	$90	$125

1958 Chevrolet Wagon, 7", made in Japan.

Good	Excellent	Mint
$60	$100	$150

Station Wagons

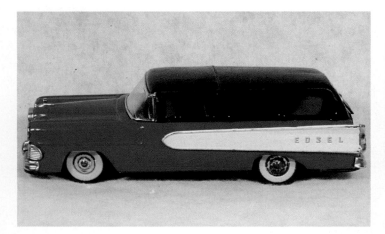

1958 Edsel Wagon, 10½", by Nomura, Japan.

Good	Excellent	Mint
$150	**$200**	**$300**

Falcon Station Wagon, marked "Pan American" airport service car, friction powered, 8¾", made in Japan.

Good	Excellent	Mint
$110	**$130**	**$170**

Ford Wagon, friction powered, 10", by Y, Japan.

Good	Excellent	Mint
$85	**$120**	**$145**

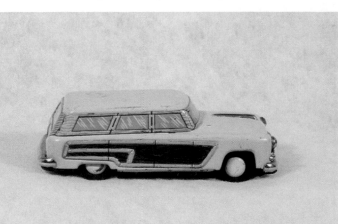

1953 Ford Woody Station Wagon, 7", made in Japan.

Good	Excellent	Mint
$90	**$110**	**$160**

1953 Ford Woody Station Wagon, marked "Flowers for Gracious Living, 7", made in Japan.

Good	Excellent	Mint
$300	**$700**	**$900**

Station Wagons

1956 Ford Wagon, 12", by Bandai, Japan.

Good	Excellent	Mint
$90	**$180**	**$250**

1956 Ford Wagon, 11¾", by Nomura, Japan.

Good	Excellent	Mint
$200	**$250**	**$350**

1956 Ford Custom Ranch Wagon, friction powered, 12", with original box. Made in Japan.

Good	Excellent	Mint
$90	**$180**	**$250**

Station Wagons

1957 Ford Wagon, 11½",
by Bandai, Japan.

Good	Excellent	Mint
$250	**$395**	**$470**

1958 Ford Woody Station Wagon,
7¾", by Bandai, Japan.

Good	Excellent	Mint
$80	**$120**	**$160**

1959 Ford Cragstan Station
Wagon, friction powered, with
original box, 13". By NGS, Japan.

Good	Excellent	Mint
$70	**$110**	**$140**

Station Wagons

1959 Ford Station Wagon, friction powered, 8³/₄", made in Japan.

Good	Excellent	Mint
$75	$100	$140

1959 Ford Station Wagon, friction powered, 10¹/₄", by Y, Japan.

Good	Excellent	Mint
$80	$110	$160

1960 Ford Station Wagon, friction powered, 10", by Y, Japan.

Good	Excellent	Mint
$80	$110	$160

1963 Ford Station Wagon, friction powered, 9³/₄", by Y, Japan.

Good	Excellent	Mint
$85	$120	$145

Station Wagons

1965 Ford Wagon, 10", made in Japan.

Good | Excellent | Mint
$80 | $120 | $150

Jeepster, 7½", made in Japan.

Good | Excellent | Mint
$100 | $150 | $175

1961 Plymouth Wagon, battery operated, mystery action, moving and blinking TV Camera, 12". By Ichiko, Japan.

Good | Excellent | Mint
$700 | $850 | $1000

Station Wagons

Plymouth Station Wagon, friction powered, 8¼", by Bandai, Japan.

Good	Excellent	Mint
$110	$150	$185

1958 Rambler Rebel Station Wagon, 11", with original box. By Bandai, Japan.

Good	Excellent	Mint
$120	$220	$300

1963 Rambler Station Wagon, friction powered, 8¼", by Haji, Japan.

Good	Excellent	Mint
$45	$95	$135

Taxicabs

Yellow Cab Co., 6½", by Arcade.

Good   Excellent
$500   **$900**

Yellow Cab Co., 9", Arcade.

Good   Excellent   Mint
$800   **$1300**   **$1600**

Yellow Taxi, 6", by Mohawk Toys.

Good   Excellent   Mint
$120   **$175**   **$230**

Taxicabs

Checker Cab Co., 6", by Chein.

Good	Excellent	Mint
$100	$150	$230

Taxicab, 6", by Orbor, Germany.

Good	Excellent	Mint
$185	$270	$345

Yellow Taxi Co., 7", by Mohawk Toys.

Good	Excellent	Mint
$110	$160	$240

Taxicabs

Yellow Taxi Main, 5¾", by Chein.

Good	Excellent	Mint
$90	**$150**	**$230**

Tricky Taxi and Fire Chief, with original box, 4½", by Louis Marx.

Good	Excellent	Mint
$60	**$125**	**$175**

1939 Charlie McCarthy and Mortimer Snerd, we'll mow you down, 16½", by Marx.

Good	Excellent	Mint
$1200	**$2500**	**$3500**

Taxicabs

Amos 'n' Andy Taxi Cab, with original box, 8". By Marx, USA.

Good	Excellent	Mint
$375	$800	$1000

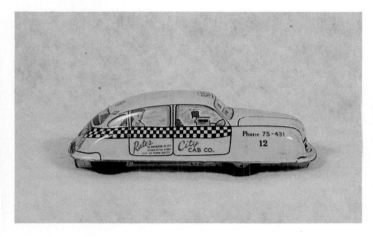

City Cab Co., friction powered, 7¹/²", by Marx, USA

Good	Excellent	Mint
$100	$130	$165

Checker Cab wind-up, 7", by General Metal Toys Ltd., Canada.

Good	Excellent	Mint
$80	$120	$155

1962 Chevrolet Taxi, friction powered, 7¹/²", made in Japan.

Good	Excellent	Mint
$90	$145	$175

1959 Buick Yellow Cab, friction powered, 8¹/²", made in Japan.

Good	Excellent	Mint
$100	$145	$175

Cast Iron Racers

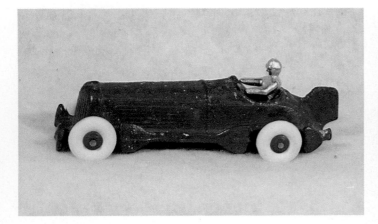

Champion Racer, 8½".

Good **$150**   Excellent **$225**

Hubley Racer, 5¼".

Good **$175**   Excellent **$225**

Hubley Racer, 7½".

Good **$60**   Excellent **$100**   Mint **$150**

Hubley Racer, 6", made in USA.

Good **$150**   Excellent **$275**

Hubley Racer, 6¾".

Good **$170**   Excellent **$250**

Hubley Racer, 9½", made in USA.

Good **$1650**   Excellent **$2000**

Cast Iron Racers

Hubley Racer, 9¹/²", made in USA.

Good   Excellent
$1650   **$2000**

Peerless Racer, 5¹/²".

Good   Excellent
$450   **$600**

Racer, 6¹/²".

Good   Excellent   Mint
$125   **S200**   **$275**

Cast Iron Racers

Racer, 6½".

Good	Excellent	Mint
$100	**$165**	**$200**

Racer, 5¼".

Good	Excellent	Mint
$100	**$165**	**$200**

Racer, 7¼".

Good	Excellent	Mint
$165	**$240**	**$290**

Racer, 6½".

Good	Excellent
$125	**$200**

German Racers

1920's 7¼" x 6½" Garage with two wind-up racers 6½", by G & K, Germany.

Good	Excellent	Mint
$1000	$1400	$1700

Racer, 8", by G & K, Germany.

Good	Excellent	Mint
$200	$300	$390

Racer, 5½", by Bing GNS, Germany.

Good	Excellent	Mint
$390	$650	$800

Racer, 4¼", by Gescha, Germany.

Good	Excellent	Mint
$100	$180	$235

German Racers

Coupe Gordon Bennett Racer, 8¼", by Guntherman, Germany.

Very Rare

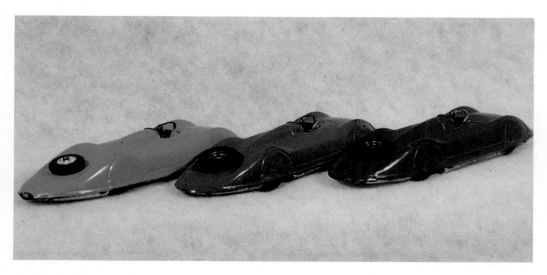

Racers, wind-ups, 4¼" long, US Zone, Germany.

Good	Excellent	Mint
$100	**$150**	**$225**

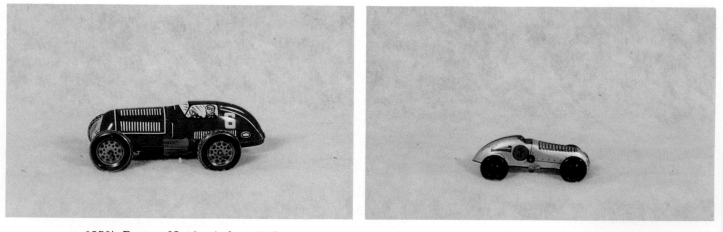

1950's Racer – No. 6, wind-up, 5½", US Zone, Germany.

Good	Excellent	Mint
$45	**$70**	**$90**

Racer – No. 1, wind-up, 3½", made in Western Germany.

Good	Excellent	Mint
$50	**$75**	**$90**

German Racers

Racer – No. 4, wind-up, 12",
made in Germany.

Good	Excellent	Mint
$675	**$1000**	**$1400**

Racers, 4¼", made in Germany.

Good	Excellent	Mint
$25	**$75**	**$100**

Race Track, 8½" x 8½", made in
Germany.

Good	Excellent	Mint
$125	**$250**	**$400**

Japan Racers

Go Stop Benz Racer, 10",
with original box, by Japan.

Good	Excellent	Mint
$200	**$300**	**$400**

1960 Chevrolet Stock Racing Car,
friction powered, 7½", with original
box. By Ichico, Japan.

Good	Excellent	Mint
$65	**$100**	**$120**

1958 Edsel pulling a Race Car,
friction powered, 11½", made in
Japan.

Good	Excellent	Mint
$140	**$185**	**$250**

Japan Racers

Ferrari Berlinetta 250/Le Mans, 11", with original box. By Asahi, Japan.

Good	Excellent	Mint
$95	$190	$275

1960's Ferrari No. 2, 8¼", by Bandai, Japan.

Good	Excellent	Mint
$85	$120	$165

1960's Ferrari No. 3, 8¼", by Bandai, Japan.

Good	Excellent	Mint
S85	$120	$165

1960's Ferrari No. 1, 8¼", by Bandai, Japan.

Good	Excellent	Mint
$85	$120	$165

1960's Ford Stock Race Car, friction powered, with original box, 11¼" long, by Tohko-Toy, Japan.

Good	Excellent	Mint
$50	$85	$110

Japan Racers

1962 Ford Galaxy Stock Racing Car, with original box, 9½" long, by TT, Japan.

Good	Excellent	Mint
$70	**$100**	**$125**

1964 Ford Stock Car, 13" long, by Ichiko, Japan.

Good	Excellent	Mint
$125	**$170**	**$225**

1965 Ford Mustang Race Car No. 12, battery operated, 13", with original box. By Yonezawa, Japan.

Good	Excellent	Mint
$150	**$230**	**$290**

Japan Racers

Lotus 49 Ford F-1, Formula Racing Car No. 36, battery operated, 16", with original box. By Asahi, Japan.

Good	Excellent	Mint
$100	**$140**	**$165**

Lotus 49 Ford F-1, Formula Racing Car No. 10, battery operated, 16", with original box. By Asahi, Japan.

Good	Excellent	Mint
$100	**$140**	**$165**

Jet Racer, 12", friction powered, by Yonezawa, Japan.

Good	Excellent	Mint
$375	**$450**	**$550**

Japan Racers

Jet Racer, 12¼",
by Yonezawa, Japan.

Good	Excellent	Mint
$375	**$475**	**$600**

1960's Plymouth Stock Car,
friction powered, 9¾" long,
by Yonezawa, Japan.

Good	Excellent	Mint
$65	**$90**	**$110**

NSU Record Racer, 12½",
made in Japan.

Good	Excellent	Mint
$80	**$150**	**$225**

Japan Racers

Roadster V-8, battery operated, 11",
with original box. By Daiye, Japan.

Good	Excellent	Mint
$90	$175	$275

Volkswagen, battery operated,
with original box, 9½", by Taiyo, Japan.

Good	Excellent	Mint
$60	$100	$145

Mercury Racer No. 55, 5½", by Marusan, Japan.

Good	Excellent	Mint
$75	$100	$150

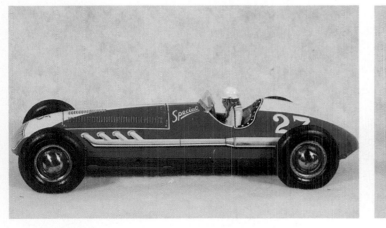

1950's Racer, friction powered, 11¼", by Marusan, Japan.

Good	Excellent	Mint
$150	$200	$290

1950's Racer, 8", by M.T., Japan.

Good	Excellent	Mint
$80	$100	$165

Japan Racers

Racer, friction powered, 8½",
by AAA, Japan.

Good	Excellent	Mint
$125	**$200**	**$250**

Demon Racer No. 7, 11¼",
made in Japan.

Good	Excellent	Mint
$60	**$95**	**$130**

1930's Prewar Racer, 6¼",
wind-up, A-1 Toys, Japan.

Good	Excellent	Mint
$230	**$325**	**$400**

Japan Racers

1960's Speed Control Racer with 5 gear shift, battery operated, 12", with original box. By Daiya, Japan.

Good	Excellent	Mint
$170	$250	$360

Break-Apart Racer, friction powered, 10³/₄", with original box. Made in Japan.

Good	Excellent	Mint
$250	$400	$550

1950's Silver Panther Racer, 11¹/₄", battery operated. By Marusan, Japan.

Good	Excellent	Mint
$150	$200	$290

Japan Racers

Red Hawk Racer, with original box, 7½". Made in Japan.

Good	Excellent	Mint
$40	$80	$95

Super Racer, friction powered, 9½", with original box. By Linemar Toys, Japan.

Good	Excellent	Mint
$130	$165	$225

High Speed Racer, marked 1908 Vanderbuilt Cup Race, friction motor, 11½", with original box. Made in Japan.

Good	Excellent	Mint
$180	$290	$350

Three Race Cars, marked "Bear, Lion, Tiger", 4", made in Japan.

Good	Excellent	Mint
$35 ea.	$60 ea.	$75 ea.

Japan Racers

Racer No. 18, 7½", by KKK, Japan.

Good	Excellent	Mint
$150	**$200**	**$250**

Comet Race Car No. 73, friction powered, 9", with original box. By Yonezawa, Japan.

Good	Excellent	Mint
$35	**$50**	**$75**

Comet Race Car No. 55, friction powered, 9", with original box. By Yonezawa, Japan.

Good	Excellent	Mint
$35	**$50**	**$75**

No. 7 Racer, tin friction powered, 5", by Yonezawa, Japan.

Good	Excellent	Mint
$45	**$80**	**$110**

Japan Racers

No. 2 Racer, 4", by Alps, Japan.

Good	Excellent	Mint
$80	**$130**	**$165**

Prop-Rod Racer, 8½", friction powered, with original box. Made in Japan.

Good	Excellent	Mint
$150	**$225**	**$275**

Comet Race Car No. 37, friction powered, 9", with original box. By Yonezawa, Japan.

Good	Excellent	Mint
$35	**$50**	**$75**

Racer #7, 5½", by TN, Japan.

Good	Excellent	Mint
$135	**$190**	**$225**

Midget Racer #63, 7", by Yonezawa, Japan.

Good	Excellent	Mint
$900	**$1750**	**$2200**

Racer #5, 7", by Yonezawa, Japan.

Good	Excellent	Mint
$800	**$1550**	**$2000**

Japan Racers

Racer #8, 7", by Yonezawa, Japan.

Good	Excellent	Mint
$800	$1550	$2000

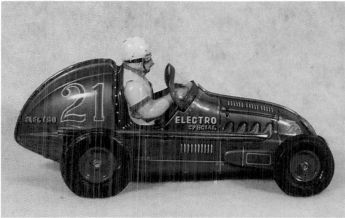

Electro Racer #21, 10", by Yonezawa, Japan.

Good	Excellent	Mint
$1475	$1800	$2450

World Speed Racer Pegasus, with original box, 11½", by Marusan, Japan.

Good	Excellent	Mint
$175	$260	$350

Taifun Race Car, friction powered, 13", by RN, Japan.

Good	Excellent	Mint
$145	$225	$300

Japan Racers

Race Car #32, battery operated, 8½", made in Japan.

Good	Excellent	Mint
$160	**$200**	**$240**

Race Car #7, 5", made in Japan.

Good	Excellent	Mint
$90	**$150**	**$275**

Atom Racer #153, 16", by Y, Japan.

Good	Excellent	Mint
$1000	**$1500**	**$1875**

Atom Jet Racer #58, 26½".
Made in Japan.

Good	Excellent	Mint
$1800	**$2800**	**$3500**

Japan Racers

Race Car #31, friction powered, 10", made in Japan.

Good	Excellent	Mint
$50	$90	$120

Race Car #10, friction powered, 9½", with original box.
By Kyowa Toy Co., Japan.

Good	Excellent	Mint
$35	$50	$75

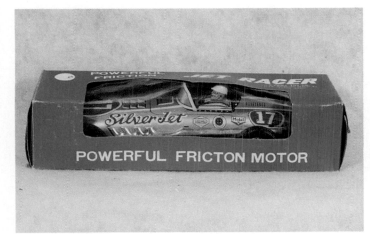

Race Car #17 Silver Jet, friction powered, 9½",
with original box. By Kyowa Toy Co., Japan.

Good	Excellent	Mint
$35	$50	$75

Race Car #99 Star, 9", made in Japan.

Good	Excellent	Mint
$100	$145	$190

Mars Jet Racer #15, 8", with original
box, by Marusan, Japan.

Good	Excellent	Mint
$150	$225	$300

Japan Racers

1955 Jet Racer, 8", with original box. By Marusan, Japan.

Good	Excellent	Mint
$175	**$250**	**$350**

Race Car #7, friction powered, made in Japan.

Good	Excellent	Mint
$50	**$90**	**$120**

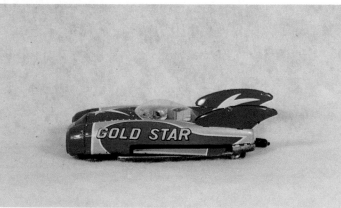

Gold Star Racer, 6¹/²", made in Japan.

Good	Excellent	Mint
$110	**$165**	**$225**

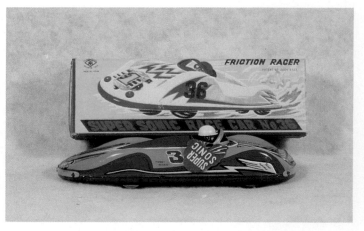

1950's Super Sonic Race Car No. 36, 9¹/⁴",
friction powered. By Modern Toys, Japan.

Good	Excellent	Mint
$90	**$120**	**$150**

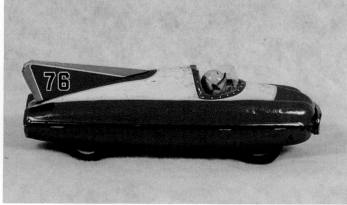

1950's Racer #76, 9", made in Japan.

Good	Excellent	Mint
$160	**$225**	**$300**

King Jet Racer, 4¹/²", friction powered, made in Japan.

Good	Excellent	Mint
$60	**$100**	**$130**

Japan Racers

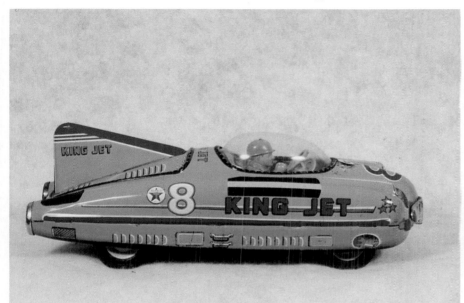

King Jet No. 8 Racer, 12¼", friction powered, made in Japan.

Good	Excellent	Mint
$250	**$350**	**$400**

Champion No. 98 Racer, 18", by Yonezawa, Japan.

Good	Excellent	Mint
$1000	**$1500**	**$2000**

Super Racer #42, 18", by Yonezawa, Japan.

Rare

Japan Racers

Agajanian Special No. 98 Racer, 18", by Yonezawa, Japan.

Rare

Fire Bird #7 Racer, friction powered, 6½", made in Japan.

Good	Excellent	Mint
$90	**$120**	**$165**

1950's Fire Bird Racer, 8½", wind-up. Made in Japan.

Good	Excellent	Mint
$100	**$185**	**$240**

Firebird Speedway Racer, 14½", by Toymania, Japan.

Good	Excellent	Mint
$150	**$200**	**$290**

Japan Racers

1961 Indianapolis 500 Racer #3, 14¾", battery operated, by Toymania, Japan.

Good	Excellent	Mint
$500	$700	$900

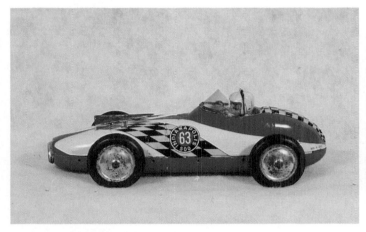

1963 Indianapolis 500 Racer #63, 9", friction powered. Made in Japan.

Good	Excellent	Mint
$250	$375	$800

1960's Ford Roll-Over Stunt Car #77, wind-up, with original box, 6½". Made in Japan.

Good	Excellent	Mint
$35	$60	$85

Stunt Car with pop-up man, 8½", friction powered, by SY, Japan.

Good	Excellent	Mint
$165	$220	$300

Japan Racers

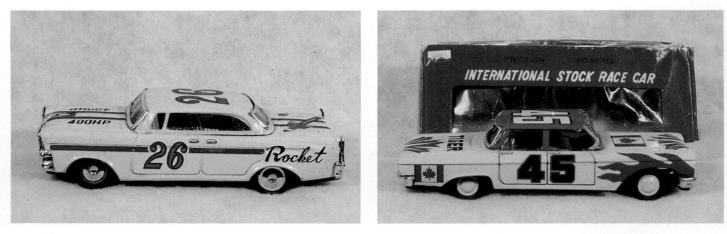

Stock Car #26, 9", made in Japan.

Good	Excellent	Mint
$40	$70	$90

International Stock Race Car, $8^{1/2}$",
friction powered, with original box, made in Japan.

Good	Excellent	Mint
$60	$90	$130

Speed King Racer, $7^{3/4}$", made in Japan.

Good	Excellent	Mint
$160	$200	$250

1960's Speed King #23 Racer, 11", made in Japan.

Good	Excellent	Mint
$45	$80	$110

U-Control Racing Car "Speed King" #7, Rosko Toy,
$9^{1/2}$", with original box. By S & E, Japan.

Good	Excellent	Mint
$200	$260	$280

Ford Stock Car #15, $8^{1/2}$", made in Japan.

Good	Excellent	Mint
$35	$55	$75

Japan Racers

1960's Racing Car Sets, made in Japan.

(Mint on Card) – **$35**

1960's Racing Car Sets, made in Japan.
(Mint on Card) – **$45**

World Champion Auto Race, wind-up cars, 9¼",
with original box. By TPS, Japan

Good	Excellent	Mint
$45	**$85**	**$140**

Prop Rod, 9¼", friction powered, made in Japan.

Good	Excellent	Mint
$100	**$150**	**$185**

Speed King Race Car, 11½", friction powered, by YA, Japan.

Good	Excellent	Mint
$100	**$200**	**$275**

Japan Racers

Indianapolis 500 Racer #1, 14¾", made in Japan.

Good	Excellent	Mint
$400	**$750**	**$900**

Speed Race Car No. 20, 6½", with original box.
Made in Japan.

Good	Excellent	Mint
$65	**$90**	**$125**

Speed Racer #25 with blinking signal lights,
battery operated, 11", with original box.
By Nomura, Japan.

Good	Excellent	Mint
$105	**$170**	**$195**

Hot Rod, 7¼", friction powered,
made in Japan.

Good	Excellent	Mint
$70	**$125**	**$185**

Japan Racers

Hot Rod, friction powered,
6½", by KD, Japan.

Good	Excellent	Mint
$75	**$100**	**$150**

Hot Rod, battery operated, 7¼",
with original box. By TN, Japan.

Good	Excellent	Mint
$75	**$125**	**$175**

Hot Rod, friction powered, 7½".
By Bandai, Japan.

Good	Excellent	Mint
$70	**$125**	**$185**

USA Tin Racers

Captain Marvel Racers, 4",
by Automatic Toy Co.,
New York.

Good	Excellent	Mint
$80	**$110**	**$150**

Auto Speedway Magic, with
original box, 10" x 18".
By Automatic Toy Co., USA.

Good	Excellent	Mint
$60	**$100**	**$150**

Custom Racer No. 15, 12³/₄",
by Brian, USA.

Good	Excellent	Mint
$100	**$160**	**$200**

USA Tin Racers

1925 Silver Dash Racer, 13¾",
by Buffalo Toys, USA.

Good	Excellent	Mint
$180	**$450**	**$700**

Racer #99, 13",
by Buffalo Toys, USA.

Good	Excellent
$300	**$700**

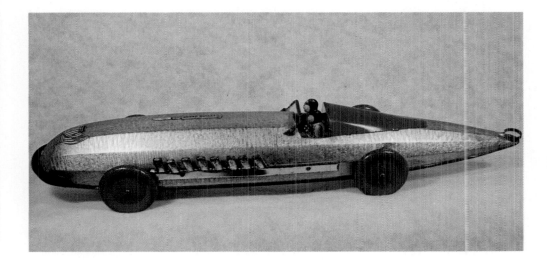

Silver Bullet Race Car, 26",
by Buffalo Toys, USA.

Good	Excellent	Mint
$225	**$375**	**$490**

USA Tin Racers

Racer #3, wind-up, 6½", by J. Chein & Co., USA.

Good	Excellent	Mint
$100	**$175**	**$250**

Racer #52, 6½", by J. Chein & Co., USA.

Good	Excellent	Mint
$90	**$140**	**$175**

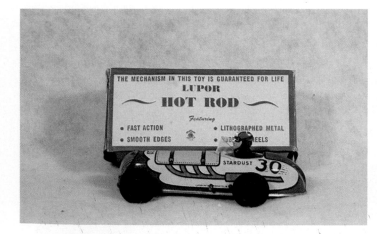

Stardust #30 Racer, wind-up, 6½", with original box, by Lupor Metal Products, New York, USA.

Good	Excellent	Mint
$50	**$85**	**$110**

Sweet Sue #96 Racer, wind-up, 6½", with original box, by Lupor Metal Products, New York, USA.

Good	Excellent	Mint
$50	**$85**	**$110**

The Race Master #8, with original box, 11". By Lupor Metal Products, New York, USA.

Good	Excellent	Mint
$75	**$110**	**$150**

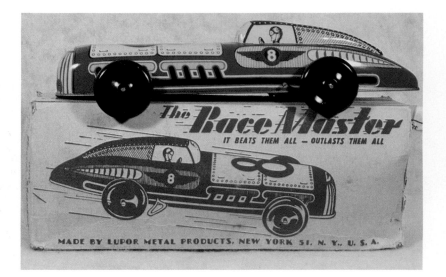

USA Tin Racers

Racer #18 Moonbeam, 6½",
by Lupor Metal Products,
New York, USA.

Good	Excellent	Mint
$100	$140	$170

Daredevil Motor Drome & Car,
wind-up, 9½" across, with original
box. By Marx, USA.

Good	Excellent	Mint
$110	$160	$200

Sparks Racer, wind-up, 8½",
by Marx, USA.

Good	Excellent	Mint
$300	$490	$700

1940's Speedway Racers, 4",
with original box. By Marx, USA.

Good	Excellent	Mint
$30	$50	$75

USA Tin Racers

1930's Racer #2, wind-up, 13¼",
by Marx, USA.

Good	Excellent	Mint
$160	**$220**	**$300**

Racer, wind-up, 13¼",
by Marx, USA.

Good	Excellent	Mint
$100	**$185**	**$250**

1930's Racer #711, wind-up,
13¼", by Marx, USA.

Good	Excellent	Mint
$100	**$185**	**$250**

USA Tin Racers

Race Cars, 5",
by Marx, USA.

Good	Excellent	Mint
$50	$75	$125

Race Cars, 5", by Marx, USA.

Good	Excellent	Mint
$50	$75	$125

Racer #14, wind-up, 6½", by Mohawk Toy Co., USA.

Good	Excellent	Mint
$90	$190	$250

USA Tin Racers

Bear Cat Racer with Garage,
both are 6³/₄", wind-up, made in USA.

Good	Excellent	Mint
$175	**$300**	**$375**

Racer, wind-up, 2³/₄",
made in USA.

Good	Excellent	Mint
$20	**$35**	**$50**

Racer, 9¹/₂", made in USA.

Good	Excellent	Mint
$150	**$250**	**$300**

USA Tin Racers

Racer #21, wind-up, 7", made in USA.

Good	Excellent	Mint
$90	$150	$200

Speedway Streamlined Racer, 6", with original box. By Lindstrom, USA.

Good	Excellent	Mint
$80	$120	$150

Racer, 10¼", made in USA.

Good	Excellent	Mint
$80	$110	$165

1930's Ford Racer, V-8, #52, wind-up, 6¼", made in USA.

Good	Excellent	Mint
$90	$140	$175

USA Racers

Cox Champion Thimbledrome Racer,
diecast, 9³/₄", Santa Ana, CA, USA.

Good	Excellent	Mint
$150	**$250**	**$300**

Cox Champion Thimbledrome
Racer, 9³/₄", diecast, Santa Ana,
CA, USA.

Good	Excellent	Mint
$150	**$250**	**$300**

Cox Thimbledrome Special
#1 Racer, 8¹/₂", made in USA.

Good	Excellent	Mint
$100	**$150**	**$200**

USA Racers

Cox Shrike Racer, 12¼",
made in USA.

Good	Excellent	Mint
$35	$75	$125

Cox Shrike Racer, 12¼",
made in USA.

Good	Excellent	Mint
$35	$75	$125

Racer, 8½", by Wyandotte Toys, made in USA.

Good	Excellent	Mint
$75	$160	$220

Racer, 6", by Wyandotte Toys, made in USA.

Good	Excellent	Mint
$100	$160	$220

USA Racers

1950's Racer, 12", diecast, Cleveland.

Good	Excellent	Mint
$145	**$200**	**$250**

Indianapolis 500 Racer, 16", by Sturm, USA.

$1000 – Mint

Racer #2, 16", by Sturm, USA.

$1000 – Mint

USA Racers

Conquer Racer #5, 18½",
Tom Sturm Special, USA.

$3500

Racer, 7", by Renwall.

Good	Excellent	Mint
$50	**$100**	**$150**

Racer, 7", by Renwall, USA.

Good	Excellent	Mint
$150	**$200**	**$300**

USA Racers

Ply. Super Bird, 9", by
Kenner Products.

Good	Excellent	Mint
$25	**$50**	**$75**

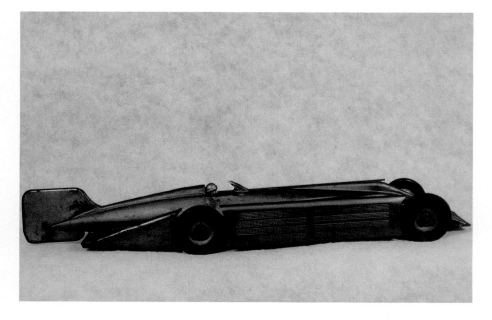

Kingsbury Racer, 20", USA.

Good	Excellent	Mint
$300	**$600**	**$900**

Sunbeam Kingsbury Racer, 19".

Good	Excellent	Mint
$950	**$1500**	**$2000**

USA Racers

Kingsbury Racer, 18½", USA.

Good	Excellent	Mint
$600	**$1000**	**$1600**

Kingsbury Racer, 20", USA.

Good	Excellent	Mint
$300	**$600**	**$900**

1950's Race Car, 7¾", by Marx, USA.

Good	Excellent	Mint
$45	**$65**	**$85**

USA Racers

1950's Midget Racer, mechanical, with original box, 6¼", by Marx Toys, USA.

Good	Excellent	Mint
$40	$60	$80

Racer #410, wind-up, 11".

Good	Excellent	Mint
$175	$250	$350

Hudson Super Six Racer, wood, 37".

Good	Excellent
$600	$1000

Racer with original box, marked "Hot See Motor", 9¾", by Nosco, USA.

Good	Excellent	Mint
$50	$90	$120

USA Racers

Willard Racer, plastic, in original case. By Strombecker.

Good	Excellent	Mint
$65	$90	$125

Two Racers, both are 4¾", by Thomas Toys, USA.

Good	Excellent	Mint
$25	$40	$60

1940's Wilbur Shaw Racer, 8½", diecast, marked Indianapolis Motor Speedway.

Good	Excellent	Mint
$120	$185	$250

Racer, 8¾", USA.

Good	Excellent	Mint
$50	$80	$120

Racer, 17½", marked Elmer's Pedal Cars – #25. Made in USA.

Good	Excellent	Mint
$1000	$1500	$2000

Cox Champion Racer, gas powered,
factory cut-a-way, 9¼", USA.

$1000

Cox Thimbledome Special TD Racer,
8½", USA.

Good	Excellent	Mint
$125	**$175**	**$250**

Slush Cast Racer with removable
hood, 4¼", USA.

Good	Excellent	Mint
$40	**$80**	**$120**

Inflatable Racer, 20½", by Bandai,
Japan.

Good	Excellent	Mint
$20	**$35**	**$50**

Aluminum Racer, 11", Cincinnati,
OH, USA.

Good	Excellent	Mint
$300	**$400**	**$500**

USA Racers

Junior Auto Race Game,
11½" x 11½", All-Fair Toys.

Good	Excellent	Mint
$45	$80	$120

Whee Whiz Auto Racer, 13" across,
wind-up, by Louis Marx & Co., N.Y.
USA.

Good	Excellent	Mint
$225	$460	$635

Straightaway, an exciting
auto racing game, 9½" x 18"
by Selchow and Righter Co.,
USA.

Good	Excellent	Mint
$30	$60	$100

USA Racers

1990 Lithuania Racer, gas powered, 16".

$2000

Grand Prix Racing, 16½", made in England.

Good	Excellent	Mint
$65	**$125**	**$200**

Ferrari Racing Car, 4" long, with original box, by Dinky Toys.

Good	Excellent	Mint
$20	**$40**	**$65**

Ferrari Race Car, 5¾" long, made in England.

Good	Excellent	Mint
$70	**$120**	**$150**

Miscellaneous Racers

French Racers, complete set, 10½", with original box.

$75 set

Racer #36, 14¼", made in France.

Good	Excellent	Mint
$300	**$400**	**$500**

Automatic Toll Gate, wind-up action, 15¼", made in Japan.

Good	Excellent	Mint
$140	**$250**	**$300**

Delivery Trucks

Packard Dump Truck, cast iron, 28", by Turner, made in USA.

Good	Excellent
$450	**$800**

Dump Truck, wind-up, 9¾", German.

Good	Excellent	Mint
$450	**$650**	**$775**

Dump Truck, 10¾", marked Sand-Gravel Metalcraft, St. Louis. Made by Metalcraft, USA.

Good	Excellent	Mint
$180	**$250**	**$300**

Delivery Trucks

Dump Truck, 11¼", marked Coke on bed of truck. By Marx, USA.

Good	Excellent	Mint
$95	$135	$170

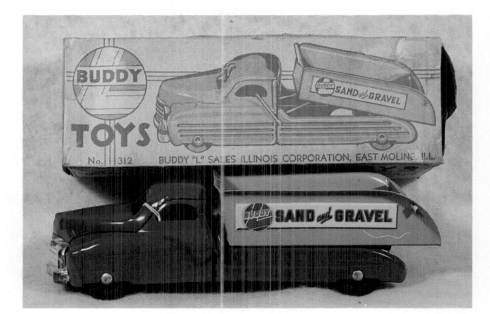

Dump Truck, 13", marked Sand and Gravel, with original box, by Buddy L, USA.

Good	Excellent	Mint
$90	$160	$225

Dump Truck, 12", marked Sand-Gravel" with original box that is marked Banner Dump Truck No. 670. By Banner Toys, USA.

Good	Excellent	Mint
$100	$145	$175

Delivery Trucks

Delivery Truck, 16½", marked
Inter-City Delivery Service, by
Lumar, USA.

Good	Excellent	Mint
$100	**$150**	**$185**

Pickup Truck, 13", marked
Firestone, made in USA.

Good	Excellent	Mint
$150	**$250**	**$350**

Fliver Model T Pickup, 12",
by Buddy L, USA.

Good	Excellent	Mint
$700	**$1000**	**$1500**

Delivery Trucks

Stake Truck, 9¾", with working headlights. By Wyandotte, USA.

Good	Excellent	Mint
$110	$150	$220

Delivery Truck, 13" long, marked Marshall's Drug Stores, USA.

Good	Excellent	Mint
$115	$190	S250

Delivery Truck, marked Meadow Brook Dairy, 10", by Metal Craft

Good	Excellent	Mint
$120	$200	$250

Delivery Trucks

Delivery Truck, marked Marcrest Dairy, 14", by Marx, USA.

Good	Excellent	Mint
$110	**$150**	**$175**

Circus Truck & Wagon, 20", by Wyandotte.

Good	Excellent	Mint
$500	**$700**	**$950**

Truck with cage on back, marked Jungle Wagon, 11½", by Nylint.

Good	Excellent	Mint
$80	**$125**	**$175**

Delivery Trucks

Easter Truck, 10¼",
by Metal Craft.

Good	Excellent	Mint
$75	$200	$350

Delivery Truck with electric lights,
rubber tires, all steel body. Advertising
Heinz 57 Products, with original box.
Made in USA.

Good	Excellent	Mint
$350	$600	$850

Dump Truck, 18", by Structo, USA.

Good	Excellent	Mint
$100	$150	$250

Delivery Trucks

White 3000 Semi, 13", with
original box. By Topping Models,
USA.

Good	Excellent	Mint
$100	**$220**	**$300**

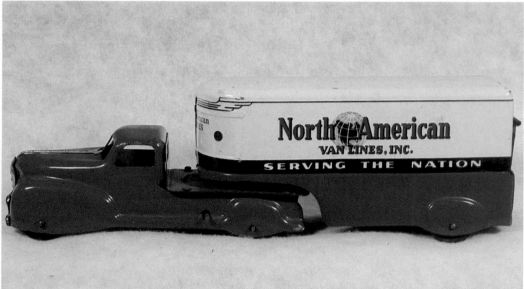

North American Van Lines
Truck, 13³/₄", made in USA.

Good	Excellent	Mint
$110	**$190**	**$250**

Hi Way Express Semi, 16" long,
by Marx, USA.

Good	Excellent	Mint
$50	**$125**	**$250**

Delivery Trucks

Panel Dodge Truck, 5½", made in Japan.

Good	Excellent	Mint
$45	**$60**	**$85**

City Delivery Panel Truck, 11", made in USA.

Good	Excellent	Mint
$100	**$150**	**$220**

Gas Truck, 10½", by Wyandotte, USA.

Good	Excellent	Mint
$90	**$110**	**$160**

Delivery Trucks

Gas Truck, 10½", by Wyandotte, USA.

Good	Excellent	Mint
$90	**$110**	**$160**

Gas Truck, 15", marked Pure, The Pure Oil Co., made in USA.

Good	Excellent	Mint
$550	**$750**	**$1000**

Delivery Truck (one of a kind), 7", by Heinz, USA.

$50

Delivery Trucks

Delivery Wagon, marked Toy Town Delivery, 21" long, by Wyandotte Toys, USA.

Good	Excellent	Mint
$270	$350	$495

Delivery Truck, 11", marked Toy Town Grocery, by Metal Craft.

Good	Excellent	Mint
$250	$450	$650

Toy Town Express Van Lines, Deluxe Service, 12" long, by Marx.

Good	Excellent	Mint
$50	$125	$250

Delivery Trucks

Package Delivery Truck, 12",
marked Wyndot Package Delivery.
By Wyandotte, made in USA.

Good	Excellent	Mint
$50	$125	$250

Delivery wind-up, 5¼", by
G & K, Germany.

Good	Excellent	Mint
$350	$490	$700

Express Truck, 5¾", by Orobr,
Germany.

Good	Excellent	Mint
$290	$450	$600

Cragstan Milk, 4¾", made in
Japan.

Good	Excellent	Mint
$70	$100	$120

Delivery Trucks

Milk Truck, 5", made in Japan.

Good	Excellent	Mint
$65	$80	$90

Gorden's Farm Products Milk Truck, 3 1/2", by MSK, Japan.

Good	Excellent	Mint
$90	$130	$150

Corvair Van, Bell Telephone Company, friction powered, 8". by KTS, Japan.

Good	Excellent	Mint
$80	$110	$150

Parcel Delivery, slush, cast, 3 5/8".

Good	Excellent	Mint
$30	$75	$100

Railway Express, 16", by Buddy L, USA.

Good	Excellent	Mint
$375	$550	$1000

Delivery Trucks

Wagon Truck, marked "Ol' Buddy's Pie Wagon", made of sturdy steel, 10", made by Buddy L, USA.

Good	Excellent	Mint
$50	**$70**	**$100**

U.S. Fish Hatchery Truck, 10", by Hubley, USA.

Good	Excellent	Mint
$50	**$90**	**$125**

Delivery Truck for Coca-Cola, 11¼", by Metal Craft.

Good	Excellent	Mint
$425	**$650**	**$850**

Emergency Vehicles

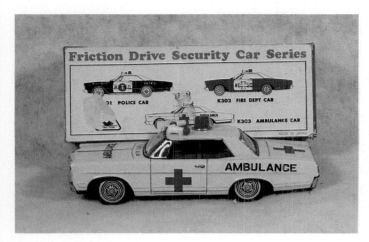

Ford Ambulance, friction powered, 8", with original box, by Bandai, Japan.

Good	Excellent	Mint
$80	$115	$140

1963 Ford Ambulance, 10½", made in Japan.

Good	Excellent	Mint
$30	$70	$90

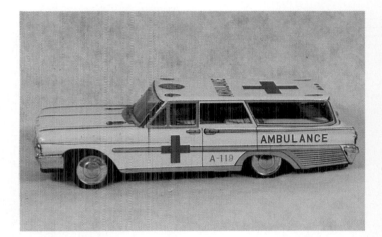

1956 Ford Ambulance, 11", friction powered, with original box. By Bandai, Japan.

Good	Excellent	Mint
$200	$300	$450

Emergency Vehicles

1959 Buick Firechief Car, 8³/₄",
friction powered, by Y, Japan.

Good	Excellent	Mint
$90	**$110**	**$140**

1961 Buick Fire Chief Car, 7¹/₄",
friction powered, made in
Japan.

Good	Excellent	Mint
$50	**$100**	**$140**

1961 Buick Fire Chief Car,
16", by TN, Japan.

Good	Excellent	Mint
$225	**$300**	**$375**

1963 Chevrolet Fire Chief Car,
13³/₄", made in Japan.

Good	Excellent	Mint
$75	**$120**	**$180**

Emergency Vehicles

1961 Mustang GT Fire Chief Car, friction powered, 15¹⁄²", with original box. By TN, Japan.

Good	Excellent	Mint
$225	$350	$450

Mercedes-Benz Fire Chief Car, 14¹⁄⁴", friction powered, with original box. By TN, Japan.

Good	Excellent	Mint
$110	$200	$240

1958 Oldsmobile Fire Chief, 8", friction powered, with original box. Made in Japan.

Good	Excellent	Mint
$75	$120	$150

1958 Oldsmobile Fire Chief Wagon, 7¹⁄⁴", with original box. By TN, Japan.

Good	Excellent	Mint
$75	$100	$130

Emergency Vehicles

Fire Chief Car, battery operated, 12½", by Taiyo, Japan.

Good	Excellent	Mint
$100	**$150**	**$200**

Fire Chief Car, battery operated with mystery action, 9¾", with original box. By TN, Japan.

Good	Excellent	Mint
$90	**$140**	**$200**

Fire Dept. Car, 7", with original box, by Bandai, Japan.

Good	Excellent	Mint
$80	**$120**	**$155**

Emergency Vehicles

Fire Chief Car, 14½", by Hoge
Mfg., Co., USA.

Good	Excellent	Mint
$200	**$325**	**$425**

Hook and Ladder, (Snoopy & Gus),
7½", by Marx, USA.

Good	Excellent	Mint
S500	**$850**	**$1000**

Fire Chief Car, wind-up, 7¹,
by Courtland Toys, USA.

Good	Excellent	Mint
$65	**$80**	**$120**

Fire Truck, cast iron, 4½".

Good	Excellent	Mint
$110	**$140**	**$175**

Emergency Vehicles

Fire Truck with 6" ladders,
8½", cast iron.

Good	Excellent	Mint
$350	**$500**	**$700**

Fire Truck cast iron, 5¼".

Good	Excellent
$125	**$250**

Fire Truck cast iron, 4¾".

Good	Excellent
$125	**$225**

Fire Truck cast iron, 5".

Good	Excellent	Mint
$120	**$165**	**$190**

Arcade Fire Truck cast
iron, with ladders, 11".

Good	Excellent
$220	**$450**

Emergency Vehicles

Fire Truck cast iron, 6½".

Good   Excellent
$125   **$225**

Fire Truck cast iron, 12".
Ladders are 8½". By
Kenton Toy.

Good   Excellent   Mint
$500   **$850**   **$1100**

Mack Fire Truck, cast iron,
18", with ladders.

Good   Excellent   Mint
$500   **$1400**   **$2500**

Emergency Vehicles

Fire Truck, 19", by
Anotherwood Toy, Canada.

Good	Excellent	Mint
$125	**$200**	**$250**

Keystone Fire Truck,
Combination 49 Fire Dept.,
cast iron, 28½", made in USA.

Good	Excellent
$700	**$1100**

Fire Truck cast iron, 21", with
ladders. By Structo, USA.

Good	Excellent	Mint
$150	**$350**	**$450**

Emergency Vehicles

Cadillac Police Car, 9¾",
by SSS, Japan.

Good   Excellent   Mint
$65   **$110**   **$140**

1960 Cadillac Police Patrol Car,
18", by SSS, Japan.

Good   Excellent   Mint
$500   **$1000**   **$1400**

1960 Cadillac Polizei Car,
friction powered with siren,
6¼", with original box. By
ICHIKO, Japan.

Good   Excellent   Mint
$65   **$90**   **$140**

Emergency Vehicles

1963 Chevrolet Police Car,
friction powered, 17½",
by TN, Japan.

Good	Excellent	Mint
$90	$200	$300

1963 Chevrolet Highway Patrol
Car, battery operated, 14", with
original box. Made in Japan.

Good	Excellent	Mint
$90	$140	$210

1963 Chevrolet Unmarked
Secret Agents Car with Mystery
Action, battery operated, 14¼", with
original box, by Spesco, Japan.

Good	Excellent	Mint
$100	$165	$200

Emergency Vehicles

1963 Chevrolet Highway
Patrol, 13³/₄", by Yonezawa,
Japan.

Good	Excellent	Mint
$55	**$100**	**$150**

Corvair Patrol Car, 9¹/₄",
by Ichiko, Japan.

Good	Excellent	Mint
$35	**$70**	**$110**

Corvair Patrol Car, 9",
made in Japan.

Good	Excellent	Mint
$50	**$100**	**$135**

1958 Edsel Police Car,
5¹/₄", made in Japan.

Good	Excellent	Mint
$35	**$50**	**$70**

Emergency Vehicles

1958 Ford Highway Patrol, 12",
battery operated, with original
box. By Yonezawa, Japan.

Good	Excellent	Mint
$165	$225	$290

1959 Ford Highway Patrol, 9¼",
by Toymaster, Japan.

Good	Excellent	Mint
$30	$65	$85

1963 Ford Highway Patrol,
9¾", friction powered, by ASC,
Japan.

Good	Excellent	Mint
$90	$120	$165

1963 Ford Military Police,
10¾", friction powered, by
Taiyo, Japan.

Good	Excellent	Mint
$85	$120	$165

Emergency Vehicles

1965 Mustang GT Highway Patrol, 15½", friction powered, with original box. By TN, Japan.

Good	Excellent	Mint
$200	**$300**	**$390**

Ford Station Wagon Highway Patrol, 8", friction powered, with original box, by S.N., Japan.

Good	Excellent	Mint
$60	**$85**	**$110**

1960 Oldsmobile Highway Patrol Car, 9", friction powered with siren, with original box. By TN, Japan.

Good	Excellent	Mint
$80	**$125**	**$190**

Porsche, German Police Car, marked Polizei, 10½", by Distler, Belgium.

Good	Excellent	Mint
$350	**$575**	**$700**

Emergency Vehicles

Police Car with siren, 11", tin, prewar, made in Japan.

Good	Excellent	Mint
$2650	**$3300**	**$4000**

Police Car, 8", by TN, Japan.

Good	Excellent	Mint
$50	**$75**	**$125**

Police Patrol Wagon, cast iron, 16½", by Structo, USA.

Good	Excellent	Mint
$450	**$700**	**$850**

Emergency Vehicles

Police Patrol 3rd Precinct, 10", tin, by Marx, USA.

Good	Excellent	Mint
$250	**$550**	**$850**

Baby Car Set, each car is 1½", with original 4¼"box, made in Japan.

Set with box $40

Police Vehicles set, 5" x 8", by Quality Toys, Japan.

Set in package $125

Emergency Vehicles

1958 Edsels, each car is 5¼",
set of three cars with original box.
By AHI, Japan.

Good	Excellent	Mint
$35	**$65**	**$100**

Note: **Boxed set is $500**

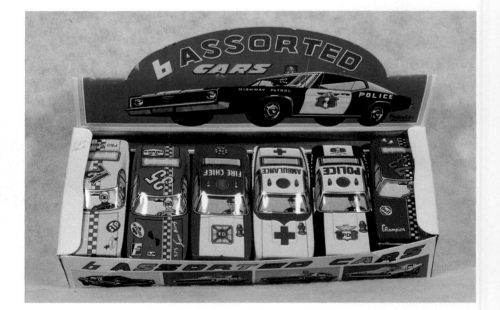

Set of 6 Assorted Cars with
original box. Made in Japan.

Set with box $150

Highway Cars set of 6,
made in Japan.

$180

Public Transportation

New York to San Francisco Bus, 21½", cast iron, by Wyandotte, USA.

Good   Excellent
$300   **$700**

Schieble's Hill Climber, Inter City Bus No. 110, 21", American Toys, USA.

Good   Excellent
$300   **$700**

Cast Iron Bus, 28" long, by Buddy L, USA.

Good   Excellent
$2800   **$4000**

Public Transportation

Greyhound Bus, cast iron, 18¼",
by Keystone, USA.

Good	Excellent	Mint
$200	**$350**	**$500**

Greyhound Bus, for The
World's Fair, Chicago
1933, 11½", cast iron.

Good	Excellent	Mint
$175	**$325**	**$400**

Faegol Safety Coach, 12½",
cast iron, by Arcade.

Good	Excellent	Mint
$500	**$650**	**$900**

Public Transportation

The American De Luxe Bus,
26½", cast iron, by Dayton
Friction Toy Co., USA.

Good   Excellent
$300   **$650**

Bus De Luxe #105, wind-up,
13", by Strauss, USA.

Good   Excellent   Mint
$300   **$500**   **$650**

Junior Bus #219, 9" long,
by Chein, USA.

Good   Excellent Mint
$225   **$350**   **$430**

Public Transportation

Military Bus, U.S. Navy, 11", with original box. By Yonezawa, Japan.

Good	Excellent	Mint
$90	$125	$160

Air Port Limousine Bus, 9", with original box, by H, Japan.

Good	Excellent	Mint
$75	$100	$130

Double Decker Bus, 7½", friction powered, by Y, Japan.

Good	Excellent	Mint
$100	$150	$200

Public Transportation

Corvair School Bus, 3", friction powered, by KTS, Japan.

Good	Excellent	Mint
$85	$120	$150

Crown Bus, 14", battery operated, with original box. By Alps, Japan.

Good	Excellent	Mint
$120	$200	$350

Royal Blue Line Bus, Coast to Coast Service, 18¼", by Chein, USA.

Good	Excellent	Mint
$700	$1200	$1550

Public Transportation

Continental Trailways Silver
Eagle Bus, 7", with original box.
Made in Japan.

Good	Excellent	Mint
$40	$60	$80

Trailways Bus, 10½", battery
operated, with original box.
By Charmy Toy, Japan.

Good	Excellent	Mint
$60	$75	$125

1950's RCA TV Bus, 8½",
made in Japan.

Good	Excellent	Mint
$60	$100	$150

Public Transportation

Street Car Trolley, 6",
wind-up.

Good	Excellent	Mint
$240	**$350**	**$490**

Bus, 12½", wind-up, by
Girard Toys, USA.

Good	Excellent	Mint
$150	**$200**	**$290**

Royal Bus Line, 9¾",
by Marx, USA.

Good	Excellent	Mint
$190	**$330**	**$390**

Public Transportation

Interstate Bus, 9³/₄",
by Strauss, USA.

Good	Excellent	Mint
$550	$700	$900

Antique Autobus, 12",
friction powered, with
original box. By SSS,
Japan.

Good	Excellent	Mint
$90	$125	$160

Blue Ribbon Bus, 10¹/₄', friction
powered, battery operated
lights, with original box. By
TN, Japan.

Good	Excellent	Mint
$220	$300	$375

Public Transportation

Avenue Bus, 8³/₄", by
Yonezawa, Japan.

Good	Excellent	Mint
$175	$230	$275

Robot Bus, 14", with original box,
marked The Bus with the Mechanical Brain, made in USA.

Good	Excellent	Mint
$80	$100	$165

Volkswagen Bus, 9¹/₂", tin,
by Bandai, Japan.

Good	Excellent	Mint
$150	$200	$290

Public Transportation

Greyhound Bus Scenicruiser, 11", friction powered with siren, with original box. By TN, Japan.

Good	Excellent	Mint
$160	$200	$230

Volkswagen Bus, 7³/₄", tin, battery operated, with original box. By Bandai, Japan.

Good	Excellent	Mint
$100	$140	$190

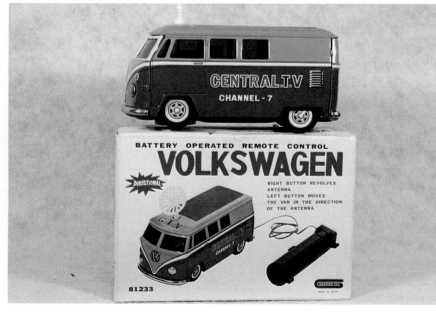

Wolkswagen Van, 7¹/₂", battery operated remote control, tin. Made in Japan.

Good	Excellent	Mint
$100	$140	$175

Public Transportation

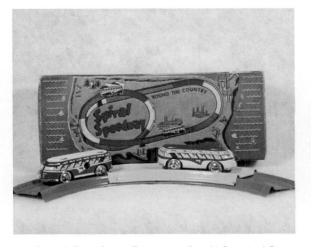

Spiral Speedway Buses, 3¾", wind-up, with original box. By Automatic Toy Co., USA.

Set with box $175

Silver Streak Streamlined Train, 13¾", with original box. Made in USA.

Good	Excellent	Mint
$45	$70	$90

Subway Express, 9¼", by Marx, USA.

Good	Excellent	Mint
$120	$220	$280

Subway with cars, 9¼", by Technofix, Germany.

Good	Excellent	Mint
$40	$70	$120

Coast to Coast Bus Line, 21", by Wyandotte, USA.

Good	Excellent	Mint
$225	$400	$500

Tonka

Custom Built Tonka, 11",
by Lennie, USA.

$200

Tonka Allied Van Lines Inc.
Semi, 23½". By Tonka, made in
the USA.

Good	Excellent	Mint
$100	**$200**	**$325**

Tonka Wrecker No. 2518,
14½", with original box, made
in USA.

Good	Excellent	Mint
$80	**$110**	**$140**

Tonka

Tonka Fire Dept. No. 5,
white set with original box, USA.

Mint $1850

Tonka State Hi-Way Dept. set with original box.
Made in USA.

Mint $1800

Tonka

Tonka Road Builder Set with original box,
made in the USA.

Mint $1400

Tonka State Hi-Way Dept. Set with original box, made in the USA.

Mint $1200

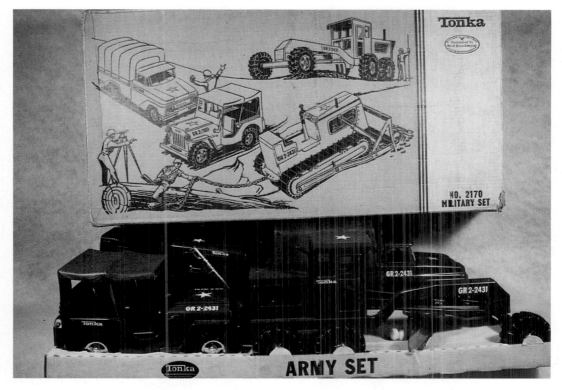

Tonka Military Set No. 2170, cast iron, with original box, made in the USA.

Mint $600

Truck Transports

Transport Automatic Car Carrier, 14", with original box. By Gescha, Western Germany.

Good	Excellent	Mint
$135	$200	$250

1959 Ford Truck Langcraft Narina Boat Carrier, 14½", friction powered with original box. By Haji Toys, Japan.

Good	Excellent	Mint
$150	$250	$350

Auto Transport, 9", the cars are 2¾", friction powered, with original box. By SSS Quality Toys, Japan.

Good	Excellent	Mint
$90	$120	$140

World Wide Automobile Carrier, 8½", the cars are 2¾", friction powered, with original box. By SSS, Japan.

Good	Excellent	Mint
$75	$90	$120

Truck Transports

Auto Transporter, 12¼", the cars are 4", friction powered, with original box. By SSS, Japan.

Good	Excellent	Mint
$85	$110	$150

1960's Cragstan Auto Carrier, 22½", friction powered, with siren, with original box. By Tohko-Toy, Japan.

Good	Excellent	Mint
$150	$290	$400

Auto Transport, 8½", made in Japan.

Good	Excellent	Mint
$65	$100	$150

Truck Transports

Motorcarrier, 13" long, made in Japan.

Good	Excellent	Mint
$110	$150	$190

Mobile Carrier, 17", with original box. By Asahi Toy, Japan.

Good	Excellent	Mint
$130	$170	$225

1959 Ford Auto Carrier with 1959 Ford Fairlane cars, 18", made in Japan.

Good	Excellent	Mint
$170	$200	$350

Truck Transports

Auto Transport with four cars, 15", battery operated remote control, with original box. By Line Mar Toys.

Good	Excellent	Mint
$115	**$145**	**$175**

Mack Truck Race Car Hauler, 22½", three race cars are 5" long, wind-up. By Marx, USA.

Good	Excellent	Mint
$900	**$1400**	**$1800**

Auto Transport with yellow cabs, 101/2", with original box. By Marx Toys, USA.

Good	Excellent	Mint
$170	**$220**	**$275**

Truck Transports

Mack Truck Race Car Hauler, 12", three red race cars are 2½" long, wind-up. By Marx, USA.

Good	Excellent	Mint
$400	**$600**	**$700**

Mack Truck Race Car Hauler, 12", three black race cars are 2½" long, wind-up. By Marx, USA.

Good	Excellent	Mint
$400	**$600**	**$700**

Mack Truck Race Car Hauler, 12", three blue race cars are 2½" long, wind-up. By Marx, USA.

Good	Excellent	Mint
$400	**$600**	**$700**

Truck Transports

Auto Transport, 32½", with friction powered cars, with original box. By Marx, USA.

Good $190 Excellent $265 Mint $400

De Luxe Auto Transport, 22", with two cars, by Marx Toys, USA.

Good $225 Excellent $340 Mint $450

Auto Transport, 23", with original box. By Marx Toys, USA.

Good $150 Excellent $200 Mint $250

Truck Transports

Auto Transport with loading ramp and three Lincolns, 28" long, cars are 6", with an original box. By Marx Toys, USA.

Good	Excellent	Mint
$250	**$350**	**$400**

Auto Transport with nine cars, 1963 Falcons, 1963 Fairlanes, 1963 T-Birds, transport is 23" long. By Sears.

Good	Excellent	Mint
$135	**$200**	**$250**

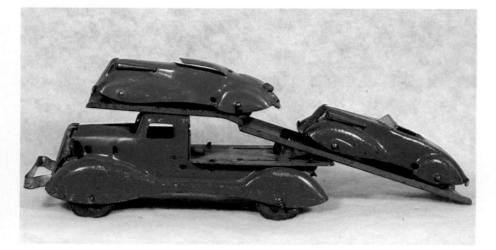

Car Carrier, 13" long, hold two cars, 6" long, made in USA.

Good	Excellent	Mint
$225	**$340**	**$390**

Truck Transports

Car Carrier, 4½", cars are 1½",
by Barclay, USA.

Good	Excellent	Mint
$50	$65	$80

Hubley Transport with four
Cadillacs, 13", made in USA.

Good	Excellent	Mint
$90	$120	$150

Car Carriers, 11" long, in original
packages. By Midgetoy, Rockford,
Illinois.

Good	Excellent	Mint
$25	$60	$80

Truck Transports

Car Carrier, 21" long,
4 cars each 6", made in USA.

Good	Excellent	Mint
$275	$390	$490

Car Carrier, 14¼".

Good	Excellent	Mint
$25	$50	$80

Auto Transport, 10" long.

Good	Excellent	Mint
$25	$40	$65

Auto Transport, 9" long,
cars are 2½" each.

Good	Excellent	Mint
$45	$90	$110

Truck Transports

Car Carrier, 21" long.

Good	Excellent	Mint
$220	$290	$375

Car Carrier, 8³/₄" long, cars are 2¹/₂".

Good	Excellent	Mint
$50	$70	$110

Auto Transport, 5" long.

Good	Excellent	Mint
$35	$45	$60

Car Carriers, 5" long,
cars are 1¹/₂".

Good	Excellent	Mint
$90	$140	$190

Trucks
Cast Iron and Pressed Steel

Lincoln Truck, Beaver Lumber Co., 17½", by Lincoln Toys, Canada.

Good	Excellent
$300	**$450**

Lincoln Truck Semi, Heinz Soups, 29", by Lincoln Toys, Canada.

Good	Excellent
$350	**$650**

Lincoln Truck Semi, Heinz Ketchup, 29", by Lincoln Toys, Canada.

Good	Excellent
$350	**$650**

Trucks
Cast Iron and Pressed Steel

Lincoln Semi Truck,
Toronto Star, 29", by
Lincoln Toys, Canada.

Good   Excellent
$400   **$800**

1957 Ford Ranchero, 11½",
by Bandai, Japan.

Good   Excellent   Mint
$200   **$325**   **$450**

International Rack Truck,
11½", by Aracade.

Good   Excellent   Mint
$500   **$750**   **$950**

Trucks
Cast Iron and Pressed Steel

Mack Truck Ice Wagon, 8¼", with ice and pick, with original box. By Arcade Toy.

Good	Excellent	Mint
$500	**$2000**	**$3500**

Ice Truck, 6¾", by Arcade Toy.

Good	Excellent	Mint
$200	**$350**	**$500**

Stake Rack Truck, 6¾", by Arcade Toy.

Good	Excellent	Mint
$175	**$450**	**$700**

Truck, 5¾", by Arcade Toy.

Good	Excellent	Mint
$270	**$300**	**$500**

Trucks
Cast Iron and Pressed Steel

International Harvester, red baby, cast iron, 10½", by Arcade Toy.

Good	Excellent	Mint
$600	$1200	$2000

White Moving Van, 13½", by Arcade Toy.

Good	Excellent
$8000	$10,000

Mack Dump Truck, 12", by Arcade Toy.

Good	Excellent	Mint
$900	$1250	$1500

Trucks
Cast Iron and Pressed Steel

Mack Gasoline Truck, 5¼", cast iron.

Good	Excellent	Mint
$120	**$150**	**$180**

Mack Truck, 4¼", cast iron.

Good	Excellent	Mint
$100	**$145**	**$175**

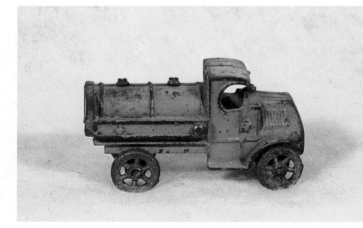

Mack Gasoline Truck, 4¼", cast iron.

Good	Excellent	Mint
$130	**$165**	**$200**

Junior Delivery Truck, 22", by Buddy L, USA.

Good	Excellent
$1650	**$2500**

Trucks
Cast Iron and Pressed Steel

Railway Express Agency Truck, 22", by Buddy L, USA.

Good	Excellent
$550	**$750**

City Special Delivery Truck, 24", by Buddy L, USA.

Good	Excellent
$450	**$750**

Truck Set No. 5860 with original box. By Buddy L, USA.

Mint $1200

Trucks
Cast Iron and Pressed Steel

Tank Line, 24½", by
Buddy L, USA

Good   Excellent
$2000 **$3000**

Shell Gas International
Truck, 29", by Buddy L,
USA.

Good   Excellent
$2500 **$4000**

Junior Tanker Truck,
24", by Buddy L, USA.

Good   Excellent
$1850 **$2500**

Trucks
Cast Iron and Pressed Steel

Express Line, 25",
by Buddy L, USA.

Good	Excellent
$1500	$2400

Coal Truck, 25", by Buddy L,
USA.

Good	Excellent
1500	$2500

Junior City Dray, 24",
by Buddy L, USA.

Good	Excellent
$1650	$2500

Trucks
Cast Iron and Pressed Steel

Railway Express Agency Truck,
21¹/₂", by Buddy L, USA.

Good	Excellent
$400	**$675**

Junior Dump Truck, 24",
by Buddy L, USA.

Good	Excellent
$850	**$1200**

Allied Van Lines Truck,
29¹/₂", by Buddy L, USA.

Good	Excellent
$350	**$700**

U.S. Mail Truck No.
2592, 22¹/₂", by Buddy L,
USA.

Good	Excellent
$325	**$600**

Trucks
Cast Iron and Pressed Steel

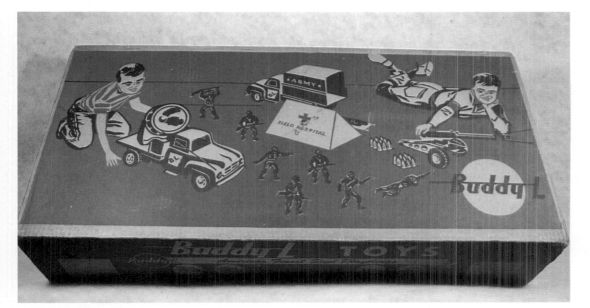

Army Supply Corps Set, with original box. By Buddy L, USA.

Mint $900

Moving Truck for La Belle, 29½", by Buddy L, USA.

Good	Excellent
$450	**$1000**

Trucks
Cast Iron and Pressed Steel

Semi Truck Curtiss
Butterfinger, 28½",
by Buddy L, USA.

Good   Excellent
$500   **$950**

Delivery Semi Truck for Snow
Crop, 23", by Dunwell, USA.

Good   Excellent
$300   **$600**

General Mack Shovel Truck,
cast iron, 10¼", by Hubley.

Good   Excellent   Mint
$250   **$475**   **$650**

Trucks
Cast Iron and Pressed Steel

Moving Van, 26", by Keystone,
USA.

Good	Excellent
$700	**$1200**

Hi-Way Express Semi, 27",
by Marx, USA.

Good	Excellent
$125	**$225**

U.S.A. 1120 Cannon Truck,
24", by Sonny, USA.

Good	Excellent
$300	**$650**

Trucks
Cast Iron and Pressed Steel

Mack Screenside Truck, 24½", by Steelcraft, USA.

Good	Excellent
$800	**$1500**

U.S. Mail Truck, 15½", by Structo.

Good	Excellent	Mint
$350	**$550**	**$700**

Traveling Store Truck, 26", by Sturditoy, USA.

Good	Excellent
$1700	**$2500**

Trucks
Cast Iron and Pressed Steel

Sturditoy Dump Truck, 27½", by Sturditoy, USA.

Good **$500** Excellent **$900**

Grey Van Lines Semi Truck, 24", by Wyandotte, USA.

Good **$175** Excellent **$375**

Richfield Gasoline Truck, 28½", made in USA.

Good **$1800** Excellent **$2500**

Trucks
Cast Iron and Pressed Steel

Sinclair Gas Truck, 17½",
USA.

Good	Excellent	Mint
$400	**$675**	**$850**

White's Dump Truck, 25½",
USA.

Good	Excellent
$700	**$1300**

Stake Truck, cast iron, 7".

Good	Excellent
$250	**$400**

Trucks
Cast Iron and Pressed Steel

Plymouth Pickup, cast iron, 4¹/₂".

Good	Excellent
$125	**$250**

Truck made of cast iron, 6¹/₄".

Good	Excellent	Mint
$165	**$250**	**$300**

Truck made of cast iron, 6³/₄".

Good	Excellent	Mint
$140	**$200**	**$240**

Truck made of cast iron, 5¹/₄".

Good	Excellent	Mint
$100	**$150**	**$225**

Trucks
Cast Iron and Pressed Steel

Truck made of cast iron, 8¼".

Good	Excellent	Mint
$170	**$330**	**$490**

Dump Truck made of cast iron, 7½".

Good	Excellent	Mint
$225	**$450**	**$600**

Truck made of cast iron, 6½".

Good	Excellent	Mint
$400	**$600**	**$750**

Trucks

Shell Gas Truck, 9¼", by
Triang, England.

Good	Excellent	Mint
$700	**$900**	**$1200**

Gama Dump Truck, 12½", made
in Germany.

Good	Excellent	Mint
$350	**$460**	**$595**

1960 Chevey Dump Truck, 9",
friction powered, with original
box. By ATC, Japan.

Good	Excellent	Mint
$60	**$90**	**$110**

Trucks

1960's Jeep with forward control, 8¼", by Bandai, Japan.

Good	Excellent	Mint
$40	$85	$125

NBC Television Camera Bus, 8½", with original box. By Cragston, Japan.

Good	Excellent	Mint
$200	$275	$350

Armored Car, 9", friction powered, with original box. By H, Japan.

Good	Excellent	Mint
$50	$85	$120

Trucks

GMC Tractor with Trailer, Allied
Moving Van, 13", friction powered,
by Line Mar, Japan.

Good	Excellent	Mint
$90	**$125**	**$175**

Judson Repair Company Truck,
15", friction powered. By Line
Mar, Japan.

Good	Excellent	Mint
$140	**$210**	**$275**

Ford Tractor with Trailer,
Koldways Refrigerated Lines,
13', friction powered. By
Line Mar Toys, Japan.

Good	Excellent	Mint
$120	**$190**	**$225**

Trucks

1957 Air Mail Truck, 8",
by Marusan, Japan.

Good	Excellent	Mint
$50	**$70**	**$85**

1950's Bell Cable Repair Truck,
11½", with original box. By
Marusan, Japan.

Good	Excellent	Mint
$65	**$100**	**$160**

Overland Transport Express,
16½", battery operated, with
original box. By Modern Toys,
Japan.

Good	Excellent	Mint
$100	**$165**	**$200**

Trucks

Dodge U.S. Mail Truck, 8½",
friction powered, by SSS, Japan.

Good	Excellent	Mint
$45	$85	$120

Left: Dodge Postal Saving
Truck, 6¾".

Good	Excellent	Mint
$30	$60	$100

Right: Dodge U.S. Mail
Truck, 8½".

Good	Excellent	Mint
$50	$100	$165

Dodge Pickup Truck, 5½", friction
powered, made in Japan.

Good	Excellent	Mint
$40	$50	$65

Truck Camper, 7½", made in
Japan.

Good	Excellent	Mint
$80	$140	$175

Trucks

Cooper-Jarrett, Inc. Freight Carrier , 6½", friction powered, with original box. By Cragstan, Japan.

Good	Excellent	Mint
$60	$100	$140

Dump Trailer, 7¾", with original box, by Cragstan, Japan.

Good	Excellent	Mint
$50	$70	$90

Sanitation Truck, 14", with original box, made in Japan.

Good	Excellent	Mint
$100	$150	$200

Trucks

Dodge Pickup Truck, 19" long, made in Japan.

Good	Excellent	Mint
$2900	$3700	$4600

Mack Dump Truck, 5", friction powered, with original box. Made in Japan.

Good	Excellent	Mint
$30	$50	$80

1960's VW's, 4", friction powered, made in Japan.

Good	Excellent	Mint
$40	$50	$65

Note: Shell add 10%

Mobilgas Tanker, 12½", made in Japan.

Good	Excellent	Mint
$100	$160	$220

Trucks

Sinclair Tanker, 12½", made in Japan.

Good	Excellent	Mint
$100	$160	$220

Maud Muller Candies Truck, 8", made in Japan.

Good	Excellent	Mint
$65	$100	$135

Junior Oil Tank Truck, 8½", by J. Chein, USA.

Good	Excellent	Mint
$300	$450	$590

Hercules Moving Truck, 7¾", by Chein, USA.

Good	Excellent	Mint
$225	$370	$480

Truckline Store Display, 6", friction powered, with original box. By Lupor, USA.
$590 for display

Trucks

Lumar Lines Sample Model
Semi, 26½", by Marx, USA.

Good	Excellent	Mint
$100	$250	$350

Dump Truck, 9½", by Marx, USA.

Good	Excellent	Mint
$175	$265	$320

U.S.A. Army Truck, 10", by
Marx, USA.

Good	Excellent	Mint
$175	$300	$390

Trucks

Dump Truck, 10³/⁴", wind-up, by Marx, USA.

Good	Excellent	Mint
$255	$300	$390

Lone Eagle Oil Co. Tanker, 12¹/⁴", By Marx, USA.

Good	Excellent	Mint
$400	$600	$875

Lone Eagle Oil Company Tanker, 12¹/²", by Marx, USA.

Good	Excellent	Mint
$400	$600	$875

Trucks

1918 Groceries Truck, 6", wind-up,
N.J., USA.

Good	Excellent	Mint
$130	**$190**	**$250**

Haul-Away- Truck, 8½",
by Strauss, USA.

Good	Excellent	Mint
$150	**$220**	**$275**

Red Star Van, 7½", wind-up,
by Strauss, USA.

Good	Excellent	Mint
$150	**$270**	**$375**

Trucks

White 3000 Truck Interstate Van,
13", by Wolverine, USA.

Good   Excellent   Mint
$200   **$250**   **$300**

White 3000 Dump Truck, 12½",
by Wolverine, USA.

Good   Excellent   Mint
$190   **$240**   **$275**

Tow Trucks

Lincoln Towing Service Wrecker,
12", by Lincoln Toys, Canada.

Good	Excellent	Mint
$90	$140	$210

Lincoln Towing Service Wrecker,
13", by Lincoln Toys, Canada.

Good	Excellent	Mint
S90	$160	$225

Dodge Wrecker, 5¹/²", friction powered,
with original box, made in Japan.

Good	Excellent	Mint
$50	$65	$85

Wrecker, cast iron, 5³/⁴", by Arcade.

Good	Excellent
$175	$250

Wrecker ride on, cast iron,
31¹/⁴", by Buddy L, USA.

Good	Excellent
$1200	$1975

Tow Trucks

Wrecker ride on, cast iron, 32", by Buddy L, USA.

Good   Excellent
$1200   **$1850**

Firestone Wrecker, 24", cast iron, by Buddy L, USA.

Good   Excellent
$500   **$900**

Wrecking Truck, cast iron, 27½", by Buddy L, USA.

Good   Excellent
$2000   **$3000**

Tow Trucks

Wrecker #5407, 14", with original box. By Buddy L, USA.

Good	Excellent	Mint
$80	$120	$160

Highway Tow Truck No. 63, battery operated, 11½", tin, with original box. By Daisy, Mfg., USA.

Good	Excellent	Mint
$90	$140	$175

Tow Truck with boom, 7½", with original box. By Hubley, USA.

Good	Excellent	Mint
$50	$85	$110

Tow Trucks

Tow Truck, 12½", by Hubley, USA.

Good	Excellent	Mint
$70	$95	$125

Tow Truck, 7", with original box, by Hubley, USA.

Good	Excellent	Mint
$50	$85	$110

Tow Truck, 7", with original box, by Hubley, USA.

Good	Excellent	Mint
$50	$85	$110

Packard Wrecker, 26", cast iron, by Keystone, USA.

Good	Excellent
$800	$1200

Tow Trucks

Ford Tow Truck for American , 11"
long, with original box. By Ny-Lint,
USA.

Good	Excellent	Mint
$60	$100	$165

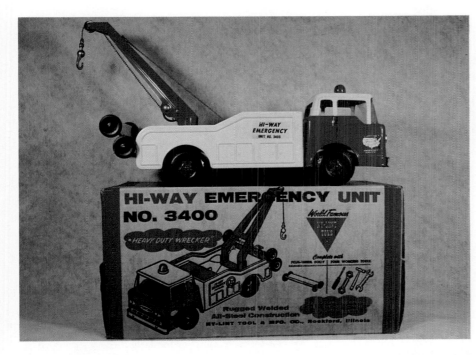

Ford Hi-Way Emergency Unit Wrecker
#3400, 18", by Ny-Lint, USA.

Good	Excellent	Mint
$110	$145	$180

Wrecker, 9", by Wyandotte,
USA.

Good	Excellent	Mint
$110	$150	$180

Tow Trucks

Wrecker, 6".

Good	Excellent	Mint
$90	**$120**	**$160**

Model A Truck with Weaver Wrecker, 11½", cast iron, by Arcade.

Good	Excellent
$600	**$1050**

Wrecker, 7", cast iron.

Good	Excellent	Mint
$190	**$250**	**$375**

Wrecker, 7¾", cast iron.

Good	Excellent	Mint
$100	**$325**	**$450**

Gas Stations/Automobile Sets

Busy Bridge, 24", by Marx, USA.

Good	Excellent	Mint
$400	$600	$800

Magic Crossroads, 18½", with original box. By Marx, USA.

Good	Excellent	Mint
$50	$90	$120

Grand Central Station, 17" x 10¾", by Marx, USA.

Good	Excellent	Mint
$85	$100	$130

Gas Stations/Automobile Sets

Highway Skill Driving, 4¼" x 13", battery operated, by K, Japan.

Good	Excellent	Mint
$70	$90	$120

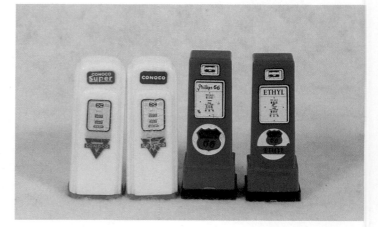

Plastic Gas Pumps, Salt and Pepper Shakers, 2¾", made in USA.

$25 a pair

Lincoln Highway Pumps, electric lighted, 91/2". Cars are 8", wind-up, by Marx, USA.

Good	Excellent	Mint
$350	$450	$600

Gas Stations/Automobile Sets

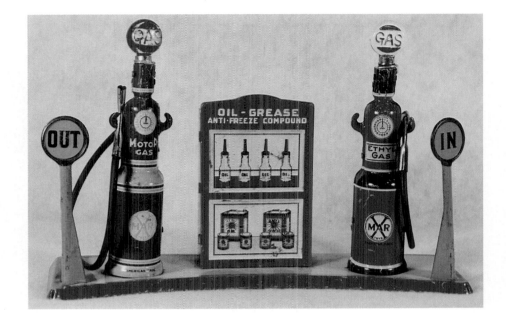

Gas Pumps, 10", by Marx, USA.

Good	Excellent	Mint
$100	**$150**	**$200**

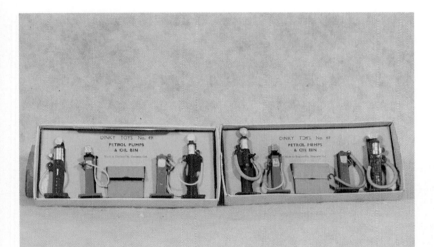

Petrol Pumps & Oil Bin No. 49,
5¾", with original box, Dinky Toys.
By Meccano Ltd., England.

Good	Excellent	Mint
$165	**$250**	**$350**

Esso Gas Pumps, 3½", with original
box, Dinky Toys. By Meccano Ltd.,
England.

Good	Excellent	Mint
$65	**$85**	**$110**

Gas Stations/Automobile Sets

Gibbs Service Station, 4½" x 7", made in USA.

Good	Excellent	Mint
$300	**$400**	**$550**

1934 Ford, World's Fair, wind-up, 7¼", prewar Japan.

Good	Excellent	Mint
$300	**$450**	**$600**

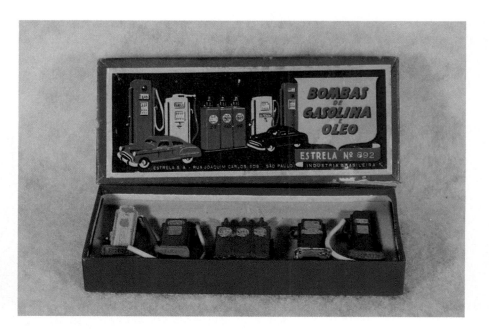

Gasoline Pumps, with original box, 6", #892, Estrela.

$245 with box

Lehmann Toys

LoLo, 4", Lehmann, Germany.

Good	Excellent	Mint
$275	$390	$490

Also, 4", Lehmann, Germany.

Good	Excellent	Mint
$300	$400	$475

Tut Tuts, 7", Lehmann, Germany.

Good	Excellent	Mint
$600	$850	$1000

Oho, 4", Lehmann, Germany.

Good	Excellent	Mint
$285	$390	$490

Motorcoach, 5", Lehmann, Germany.

Good	Excellent	Mint
$400	$690	$950

Lehmann Toys

Naughty Boy, 5", Lehmann, Germany.

Good	Excellent	Mint
$500	**$750**	**$900**

Am Pol, 5", Lehmann, Germany.

Good	Excellent	Mint
$950	**$1400**	**$1800**

Lila, 5¹/²", Lehmann, Germany.

Good	Excellent	Mint
$800	**$1100**	**$1600**

Lehmann Toys

Anxious Bride, 8½", Lehmann, Germany.

Good	Excellent	Mint
$1200	**$1650**	**$2450**

New Century Cycle, 5½", Lehmann, Germany.

Good	Excellent	Mint
$420	**$580**	**$700**

Mars Rad Cycle, 5", Lehmann, Germany.

Good	Excellent	Mint
$875	**$1200**	**$1450**

Lehmann Toys

Balky Mule, 7¹/₂", with original box, Lehmann, Germany.

Mint
$490 with box

Duo, 6³/₄", Lehmann, Germany.

Good	Excellent	Mint
$650	**$900**	**$1200**

Masuyama, 7", Lehmann, Germany.

Good	Excellent	Mint
$1000	**$1350**	**$1700**

Lehmann Toys

Masuyama, 7", Lehmann, Germany.

Good	Excellent	Mint
$1000	$1350	$1700

Ehe & Co., 6³/₄", Lehmann, Germany.

Good	Excellent	Mint
$500	$900	$1100

Galop Race Car, 5¹/₂", by Lehmann, Germany.

Good	Excellent	Mint
$400	$650	$900

Lehmann Toys

Crawling Beetle, 3³/₄", with original box, wind-up, Lehmann, Germany.

Good $85 Excellent $125 Mint $160

Paddy's Dancing Pig, 5¹/₂", by Lehmann, Germany.

Good $550 Excellent $850 Mint $1000

Zig Zag, 5", Lehmann, Germany.

Good $800 Excellent $1200 Mint $1650

Lehmann Toys

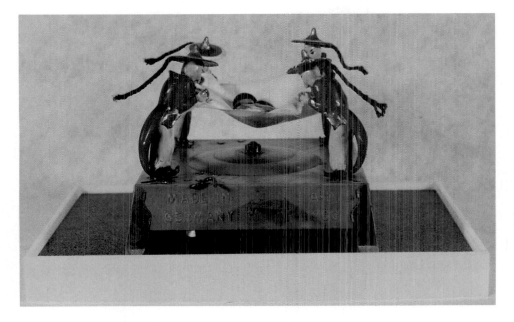

Boxer Toy, 5" x 5", wind-up, patented 1900, Lehmann, Germany.

Rare

Adam the Porter, 7¾", Lehmann,
Germany.

Good	Excellent	Mint
$800	**$1300**	**$1700**

Go Carts

Go Cart, 3½", Schuco, West Germany.

Good   Excellent   Mint
$80   **$125**   **$170**

Go Cart, 6¼", friction powered,
by Modern Toys, Japan.

Good   Excellent   Mint
$50   **$100**   **$150**

Go Cart, 6¼", friction powered,
by Modern Toys, Japan.

Good   Excellent   Mint
$50   **$100**   **$150**

Go Carts

Go Cart, 4³/₄", friction powered, by Yonezawa, Japan.

Good	Excellent	Mint
$70	**$120**	**$150**

Go Cart, 7", friction powered, made in Japan.

Good	Excellent	Mint
$70	**$120**	**$165**

Go Cart, 5", made in Japan.

Good	Excellent	Mint
$110	**$145**	**$175**

Go Carts

Go Cart, 6¼", friction powered, made in Japan.

Good	Excellent	Mint
$75	**$120**	**$160**

Go Cart, 6", engine powered, gear driven, with original box, by Herkimer, USA.

Good	Excellent	Mint
$75	**$100**	**$150**

Ice Cream Trucks

Ice Cream Truck, 6¼", by Bandai, Japan.

Good	Excellent	Mint
$70	$95	$125

Ice Cream Truck, 8", by Cragstan, Japan.

Good	Excellent	Mint
$200	$300	$375

Ice Cream Scooter, 5½", friction powered, with original box. By K, Japan.

Good	Excellent	Mint
$110	$170	$200

Ice Cream Vender, 7", friction powered, with original box. By K, Japan.

Good	Excellent	Mint
$90	$150	$250

Ice Cream Trucks

Ford Ice Cream Truck, 10¾", by KTS, Japan.

Good	Excellent	Mint
$400	$690	$850

Two Ice Cream Trucks for Good Humor, 4³/₈", by Line Mar, Japan.

Good	Excellent	Mint
$175	$320	$400

Ice Cream Panel Truck, 3¾", made in Japan.

Good	Excellent	Mint
$25	$35	$50

1960 Chevy Ice Cream Truck, 8", made in Japan.

Good	Excellent	Mint
$95	$160	$200

Ice Cream Truck, 9½", made in Japan.

Good	Excellent	Mint
$75	$175	$225

Ice Cream Trucks

Frosty Bar Ice Cream Truck, 7½", made in Japan.

Good	Excellent	Mint
$100	$150	$175

Howard Johnson Ice Cream Truck, 5½", made in Japan.

Good	Excellent	Mint
$90	$180	$210

Ford Ice Cream Truck, 8", made in Japan.

Good	Excellent	Mint
$110	$170	$220

VW Ice Cream Bus, 8¾", made in Japan.

Good	Excellent	Mint
$110	$170	$200

Walgreens Giant Ice Cream Trailer Truck, 21½", with original box, by Marx, USA.

Good	Excellent	Mint
$200	$300	$375

Aircrafts

Carnival Ride, 9", wind-up, made in Germany.

Good	Excellent	Mint
$600	$750	$900

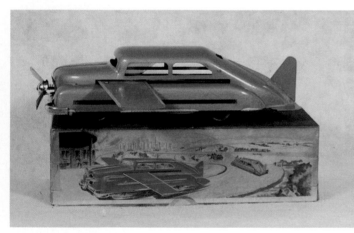

Aero-Car #500, 8", with original box, by B & S, Germany.

Good	Excellent	Mint
$350	$450	$600

Fighter Plane, 5¼" wide, by Bandai, Japan.

Good	Excellent	Mint
$80	$120	$150

Boeing 2707 SST Passenger Plane, Pan American, 7½" wing span, battery operated, with original box. By Daiya, Japan.

Good	Excellent	Mint
$75	$100	$125

Aircrafts

Boeing B-50, United States Air Force, battery operated, 14" wing span, 11" long. By Hadson, Japan.

Good	Excellent	Mint
$150	**$225**	**$300**

BK250 United States Air Force, 19" wing span, 14-1/2" long. By Y, Japan.

Good	Excellent	Mint
$220	**$300**	**$400**

F9F-5 Panther Navy Fighter Plane, 12-1/4" wing span, 12-1/2" long, friction powered. By Y, Japan.

Good	Excellent	Mint
$150	**$220**	**$300**

DC-7 Airplane, United Air Lines, 11" wing span, 9-1/2" long, friction powered. Made in Japan.

Good	Excellent	Mint
$80	**$100**	**$160**

Aircrafts

No. 63 Fighter Plane, 14½" wing span, 13" long, friction powered, made in Japan.

Good	Excellent	Mint
$350	**$475**	**$600**

Patrol Plane A-1026-S, 14" wing span, 13" long, friction powered, made in Japan.

Good	Excellent	Mint
$85	**$100**	**$140**

Passenger Plane, Capital Airlines, 14¼" wing span, 11½" long. Made in Japan.

Good	Excellent	Mint
$90	**$125**	**$175**

Aircrafts

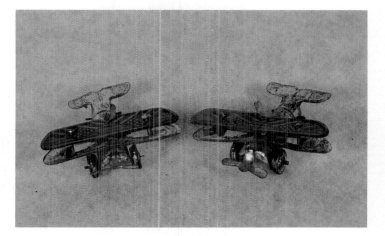

Prewar Penny Toy Airplanes. Made in Japan.

Good	Excellent	Mint
$80	$110	$150

Ford Tri-Motor Plane, 15" wing span, 11" long, friction powered. Made in Japan.

Good	Excellent	Mint
$130	$290	$400

Prewar Plane, 6", made in Japan.

Good	Excellent	Mint
$120	$190	$225

Fighter Plane with sparking machine gun, 5½" long. Made in Japan.

Good	Excellent	Mint
$60	S100	$145

Aircrafts

Helicopter, 7³/₄" wing span, 8" long, battery operated. Made in Japan.

Good	Excellent	Mint
$75	$100	$130

Skycruiser Airplane, 19" wing span, 14" long, friction powered. By Marx, USA.

Good	Excellent	Mint
$95	$130	$160

Rookie Pilot, 6³/₄", by Marx, USA.

Good	Excellent	Mint
$150	$225	$275

Aircrafts

Airplane with Pilot, wind-up, 5¼"
long, by Marx, made in USA.

Good	Excellent	Mint
$80	$120	$170

Popeye The Pilot, 7", wind-up, by
Marx, USA.

Good	Excellent	Mint
$500	$650	$750

Electra II Airplane, American
Airlines, 16½" wing span, 15" long,
battery operated. By Marx, Japan.

Good	Excellent	Mint
$75	$100	$140

Aircrafts

TWA Boeing Super Jet Plane with original box, 18" wing span, 19½" long, battery operated. By Marx, Japan.

Good	Excellent	Mint
$100	**$140**	**$190**

The Air-E Go Round 9½" high, with original box. By Reeves Mfg. Co., USA.

Good	Excellent	Mint
$260	**$325**	**$400**

Sky Rangers, 9" high base, with original box. By Unique Art Manufacturing Co., USA.

Good	Excellent	Mint
$180	**$260**	**$325**

Aircrafts

Pointed Nose Airplane with a wing span of 18", the plane itself is 12½" long. By Wyandotte, USA.

Good	Excellent	Mint
$100	**$150**	**$200**

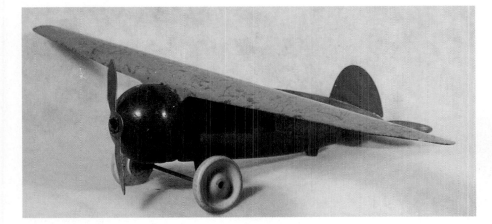

Round Nose Airplane with a wing span of 18", the plane itself is 12" long. By Wyandotte, USA.

Good	Excellent	Mint
$100	**$150**	**$200**

Flat Nose Airplane with a wing span of 18", the plane itself is 13" long. By Wyandotte, USA.

Good	Excellent	Mint
$100	**$165**	**$235**

Aircrafts

Super Jet USAF, 7", friction powered, with original box.

Good	Excellent	Mint
$45	**$80**	**$120**

U.S. Army Fighter Plane, 8" wing span, 6³⁄₄" long, wind-up.

Good	Excellent	Mint
$110	**$150**	**$225**

Zeppelin, 5" long, cast iron.

Good	Excellent	Mint
$100	**$140**	**$170**

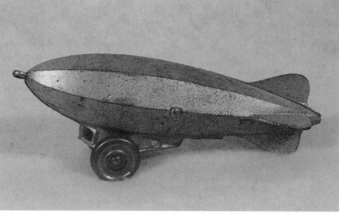

Zeppelin, 6" long, cast iron.

Good	Excellent	Mint
$100	**$145**	**$175**

Graf Zeppelin, 8¹⁄₂" long, cast iron.

Good	Excellent	Mint
$160	**$320**	**$560**

Black Memorabilia

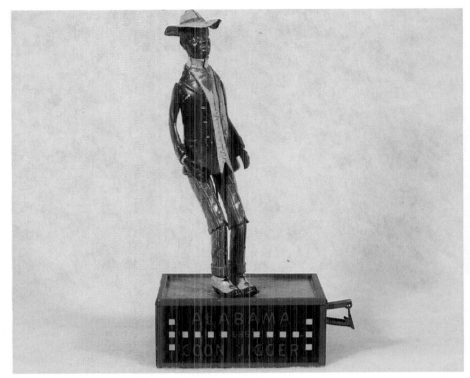

Alabama Coon Jigger, 10" high,
by Lehmann, Germany.

Good	Excellent	Mint
$400	**$550**	**$700**

Rollo-Chair riding on the boardwalk,
patented Dec. 6, 1921, 8" long. By Stock,
Germany. Imported by Strauss USA.

Good	Excellent	Mint
$800	**$1200**	**$1450**

Pango Pango African Dancer, 5¾",
wind-up, with original box. Made in
Japan.

Good	Excellent	Mint
$110	**$200**	**$230**

Black Memorabilia

Sambo with original box, 7¼",
by Alps, Japan.

Good   Excellent   Mint
$110   **$150**   **$190**

Teter-Totter, 7" x 8", wind-up,
celluloid, Occupied Japan.

Good   Excellent   Mint
$300   **$420**   **$500**

Turtle with Native Riding, 8",
by J. Chein, USA.

Good   Excellent   Mint
$95   **$140**   **$170**

Black Memorabilia

Jazzbo Jim, 5" tall, by Marx, USA.

Good	Excellent	Mint
$450	$520	$680

Bojangle Dances Again, 8 x 8½", push button, by Clown Toy Mfg. Co., Brooklyn, New York.

Good	Excellent	Mint
$90	$150	$200

Red Cap Porter, 7", wind-up, by Strauss, USA.

Good	Excellent	Mint
$500	$750	$1000

Black Memorabilia

Ham & Sam, 6½" x 5½", with original box. By Strauss, USA.

Good	Excellent	Mint
$700	**$1000**	**$1400**

Bank, cast iron, 5½".

Good	Excellent
$135	**$200**

Boats

Steam Ship Leviathan, 20",
by Bing, Germany.

Good	Excellent	Mint
$3,000	$4,200	$5,500

Steam Ship, 20" long, by
Fleishman's, Germany.

Good	Excellent	Mint
$1,000	$1,500	$2,200

Steam Ship, 10¾" long,
made in Germany.

Good	Excellent	Mint
$200	$250	$350

Boats

Neptune Tug Boat, 15", battery operated, with original box. By Modern Toys, Japan.

Good	Excellent	Mint
$80	$100	$125

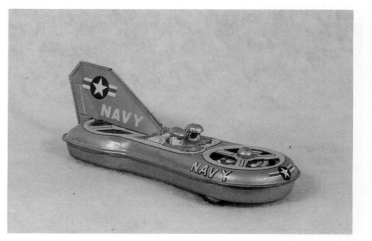

Navy Boat, 6½", made in Japan.

Good	Excellent	Mint
$60	$90	$110

Amphibious Car, 10¾", battery operated with head and tail lights, with original box. Made in Japan.

Good	Excellent	Mint
$90	$130	$165

Boats

Rowing Boat, 8" long, with original box. Made in Japan.

Good	Excellent	Mint
$165	**$210**	**$265**

Speed Boat, 16½", wind-up, by Lionel, USA.

Good	Excellent	Mint
$300	**$400**	**$525**

Cartoon and Character Toys

Harold Lloyd Bell Face, 6¼", by DRGM.

Good	Excellent	Mint
$320	$450	$550

Charlie Chaplin, 8½", wind-up, made in Germany.

Good	Excellent	Mint
$900	$1200	$1500

Felix the Cat, 6¼" tall x 8" long, wind-up, made in Germany.

Good	Excellent	Mint
$400	$700	$850

Cartoon and Character Toys

Tom and Jerry Scooter, 4¼",
friction powered, with original box.
By Marx, Hong Kong.

Good	Excellent	Mint
$40	$90	$120

Lone Ranger, 4', wind-up, made in
Japan.

Good	Excellent	Mint
$100	$175	$220

Huckleberry Hound Corvair, 9",
by Line Mar, Japan.

Good	Excellent	Mint
$150	$250	$375

Cartoon and Character Toys

Huckleberry Hound on Go Cart, 6", by Line Mar, Japan.

Good	Excellent	Mint
$300	$500	$550

Yogi Bear on Go Cart, 6", by Line Mar, Japan.

Good	Excellent	Mint
$300	$500	$550

Gumby's Jeep, 9³/₄", by Lakeside Toys, Japan.

Good	Excellent	Mint
$90	$180	$275

Cartoon and Character Toys

Monkees Mobile, GTO Barris Custom, 11¾", by ASC, Japan.

Good	Excellent	Mint
$200	$350	$450

Rubbles Wreck, 7¼", by Marx, Japan.

Good	Excellent	Mint
$300	$550	$650

Flinstone Flivver, 6½", by Marx, Japan.

Good	Excellent	Mint
$300	$550	$650

Dagwood The Driver, 8", by Marx, USA.

Good	Excellent	Mint
$600	$900	$1100

Cartoon and Character Toys

Milton Berle, 5½", wind-up, by Marx, USA.

Good	Excellent	Mint
$180	$250	$325

Tidy Tim, 9", by Louis Marx Co, USA.

Good	Excellent	Mint
$300	$500	$750

Cartoon and Character Toys

Charlie McCarthy, 8½", by Marx, USA.

Good	Excellent	Mint
$115	$170	$225

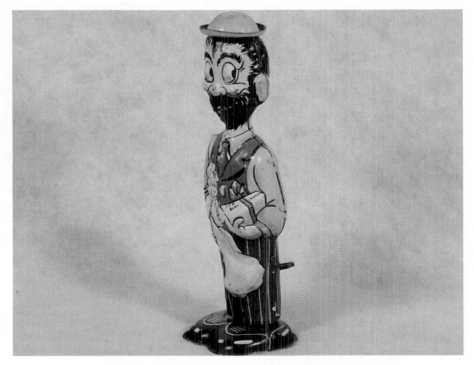

B.O. Plenty, 8½", by Marx, USA.

Good	Excellent	Mint
$90	$140	$175

Cartoon and Character Toys

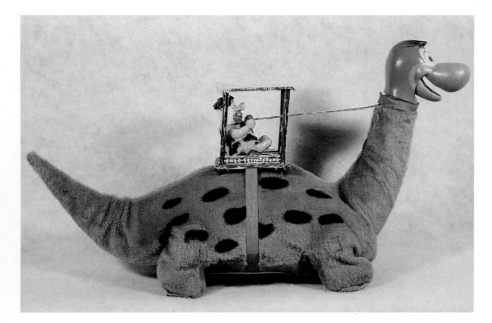

Dino The Dinosaur and Fred Flintstone, 20" tall, by Marx.

Good	Excellent	Mint
$200	**$400**	**$500**

Merry Makers, 9¹/²", by Marx.

Good	Excellent	Mint
$600	**$800**	**$1000**

Popeye Dippy Dumper, 9¹/⁴", by Marx.

Good	Excellent	Mint
$300	**$450**	**$600**

Cartoon and Character Toys

Walking Popeye, 3", wind-up, by Marx, USA.

Good	Excellent	Mint
$300	**$450**	**$700**

Popeye and Olive Oyl Jigger, 5" tall, with original box, by Marx, USA.

Good	Excellent	Mint
$800	**$1000**	**$1500**

Cartoon and Character Toys

Popeye Express with pop-up parrot, 9", wind-up, by Marx.

Good	Excellent	Mint
$480	**$650**	**$850**

1.   Popeye Paddle Wagon, 5", by Corgi.

Good	Excellent	Mint
$130	**$175**	**$225**

2.   Popeye Bisque Toothbrush Holder, 5", Chicago World's Fair 1933.

Good	Excellent	Mint
$120	**$225**	**$350**

3.   Popeye, tin, 3¾"

Good	Excellent	Mint
$10	**$15**	**$25**

4.   Popeye Big Little Book, 4½" x 3½".

Good	Excellent	Mint
$10	**$20**	**$50**

5.   Popeye Chalk-ware, 7½".

Good	Excellent	Mint
$20	**$35**	**$150**

Cartoon and Character Toys

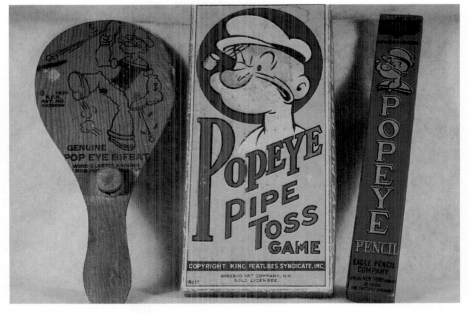

1. 1929 Popeye Bifbat, 11½".
Good	Excellent	Mint
$20	$30	$45

2. Popeye Pipe Toss Game, 5" x 11", with original box. By Rosebud Art Co.
Good	Excellent	Mint
$20	$30	$45

3. Popeye Pencil, 10¾", with original box.
Good	Excellent	Mint
$25	$40	$60

Popeye Paints, 6", with original box.
Good	Excellent	Mint
$15	$20	$30

1934 Popeye Cazoo Pipe, 3½".
Good	Excellent	Mint
$15	$20	$35

Popeye jointed, 5".
Good	Excellent	Mint
$70	$100	$130

Corn Cob Pipe, 5".
Good	Excellent	Mint
$5	$7	$10

1958 Popeye Pipe that looks lit and toots, 9½" x 5¼", with original box.
Good	Excellent	Mint
$20	$30	$50

Popeye The Boxer, 7½" x 4¾", wind-up, by Chein, USA.

Good	Excellent	Mint
$750	$1100	$1400

Cartoon and Character Toys

Tooterville Trolley, 5" x 7", copyright 1922, Fontaine Fox, by Nifty, USA.

Good	Excellent	Mint
$425	**$575**	**$700**

G.I. Joe and K-9 Pups, 9", wind-up, by Unique Art Mfg. Co., USA.

Good	Excellent	Mint
$90	**$120**	**$180**

Cartoon and Character Toys

Lil Abner Band, 9", wind-up, by Unique Art Mfg. Co., USA.

Good	Excellent	Mint
$260	**$320**	**$450**

Humphrey Mobile, 9", wind-up, by Wyandotte Toys, USA.

Good	Excellent	Mint
$300	**$440**	**$550**

Woody Woodpecker Clock, 7½", made in USA.

Good	Excellent	Mint
$200	**$350**	**$450**

The Beatles in a 1964 Ford Convertible, 18³/₄", by Rico, Spain.

Rare

Tom & Jerry Car, 1959 Oldsmobile Convertible,
13", by Rico, Spain.

Good	Excellent	Mint
$300	**$450**	**$600**

Clowns

Clown that goes in circles, 7³/₄",
wind-up, made in Germany.

Good	Excellent	Mint
$490	**$700**	**$850**

Clown Drummer, 4¹/₂" tall, wind-up,
by Schuco, Germany.

Good	Excellent	Mint
$70	**$130**	**$150**

Clown, 4³/₄", wind-up, by Schuco, Germany.

Good	Excellent	Mint
$175	**$250**	**$325**

Cragstan Melody Band Clown, 9¹/₂",
battery operated, by Alps, Japan.

Good	Excellent	Mint
$35	**$120**	**$165**

Clowns

Clown and Monkey, 10" tall, battery operated, by Alps, Japan.

Good
$140

Excellent
$200

Mint
$250

Juggling Clown, 8", wind-up, by BF, Japan.

Good
$220

Excellent
$300

Mint
$375

Clowns

Funny Rocker, prewar, 4", with original box. By Bandai, Japan.

Good	Excellent	Mint
$90	$120	$160

Clown and Monkey in a Car, 8", battery operated, by Modern Toys, Japan.

Good	Excellent	Mint
$100	$150	$200

Clown advertising "Eat At Joe's", 8", by TN, Japan.

Good	Excellent	Mint
$80	$110	$145

Clowns

Crazy Clown with Head Wind Mechanism, 4½", friction powered, with original box. By Yonezawa, Japan.

Good	Excellent	Mint
$40	**$80**	**$110**

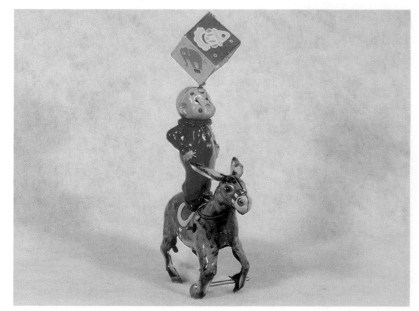

Circus Rider, 5¼" long x 8¼" high, made in Japan.

Good	Excellent	Mint
$100	**$175**	**$225**

Clown 9¼", wind-up, with original box, made in Japan.

Good	Excellent	Mint
$60	**$100**	**$135**

Clowns

Clown Magician, 6½", wind-up,
made in Japan.

Good	Excellent	Mint
$80	$140	$175

Skating Clown, 6", wind-up,
made in Japan.

Good	Excellent	Mint
$140	$200	$260

Blinky The Clown, 10" tall,
battery operated remote control,
with original box, made in Japan.

Good	Excellent	Mint
$110	$170	$225

Clowns

Funny Flivver, 7¼", wind-up,
with original box, by Marx, USA.

Good   Excellent   Mint
$340   **$420**   **$500**

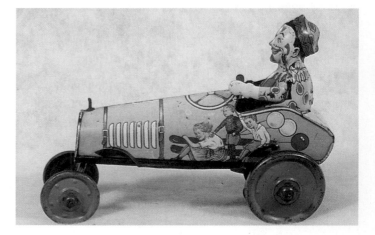

Clown Crazy Car, 7¼", wind-up,
by Unique Art Mfg. Co., USA.

Good   Excellent   Mint
$200   **$275**   **$350**

Clown Crazy Car, 7½",
by Unique Mfg. Co., USA.

Good   Excellent   Mint
$225   **$300**   **$340**

Clowns

Clown, 5¹⁄₂" tall, wind-up, by J. Chein & Co., USA.

Good	Excellent	Mint
$125	**$200**	**$240**

Banjo Player, 10¹⁄₂", wind-up.

Good	Excellent	Mint
$230	**$320**	**$375**

Clowns

Clown in Auto, 7", wind-up.

Good	Excellent	Mint
$240	**$390**	**$460**

Jumbo Eis Clown, 8¼".

Good	Excellent	Mint
$160	**$220**	**$300**

Disney

Mickey's Mail Jeep, 2¹ᐟ²', by
Matchbox, Hong Kong.

Good	Excellent	Mint
$8	$15	$20

Donald Drummer, 6" tall, wind-up,
by Line Mar Toy, Japan.

Good	Excellent	Mint
$270	$450	$550

Disneyland #6 Fire Truck,
18", with 25" ladder. By
Line Mar, Japan.

Good	Excellent	Mint
$600	$900	$1100

Disney

Disney Piston Race Car, 9¼", battery
operated, with original box.
By Modern Toys, Japan.

Good	Excellent	Mint
$50	$75	$90

Duck Riding Tricycle, 4½" long x 6" high,
all tin, made in Japan.

Good	Excellent	Mint
$180	$330	$445

Mickey Mouse Fire Truck, 6½", by Sun Rubber Co., USA.

Good	Excellent	Mint
$60	$100	$160

Mickey Mouse Race Car, 4", wind-up, USA.

Good	Excellent	Mint
$175	$250	$350

Disney

Mickey Mouse Ferris Wheel, 16½", by
J. Chein Co., USA.

Good	Excellent	Mint
$250	**$325**	**$400**

Mickey Mouse Tow Truck,
battery operated remote control,
by Andy Gard General Molds and
Plastic Co., Leetsdale, PA.

Good	Excellent	Mint
$80	**$150**	**$250**

Disneyland Rollercoaster,
10" x 19½", by J. Chein & Co.,
USA.

Good	Excellent	Mint
$300	**$450**	**$600**

Disney

Mickey Mouse Hand Car, 9½", with original box. By Lionel Corp., New York, USA.

Good	Excellent	Mint
$275	$400	$550

Donald Duck Crazy Car, 5½", by Marx, USA.

Good	Excellent	Mint
$300	$400	$450

Figaro from the story of Pinocchio, 4¾", wind-up, by Marx, USA.

Good	Excellent	Mint
$70	$100	$130

Disney

Donald Duck Duet, 10" high, wind-up,
by Marx, USA.

Good	Excellent	Mint
$300	$550	$650

Mickey Mouse, 7", wind-up,
by Marx.

Good	Excellent	Mint
$80	$120	$175

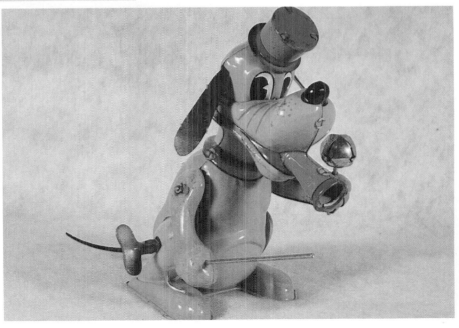

Pluto The Drum Major, 6¼",
wind-up, by Marx, USA.

Good	Excellent	Mint
$220	$275	$450

Disney

1939 Pluto "Watch Me Roll Over", 8",
wind-up, by Marx, USA.

Good   Excellent   Mint
$150   **$200**   **$275**

1939 Pluto (push tail down to go),
10", by Marx, USA.

Good   Excellent   Mint
$125   **$200**   **$300**

Mickey and Minnie Car, 6½",
by Marx, USA.

Good   Excellent   Mint
$290   **$360**   **$400**

Disney

Musical Pluto, 8" x 8", by Marx.

Good | Excellent | Mint
$350 | **$600** | **$700**

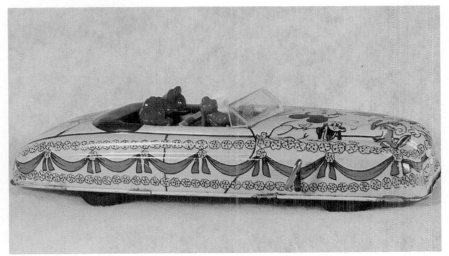

Disney Parade Car, 11", by Marx.

Good | Excellent | Mint
$150 | **$300** | **$400**

Play Block with Mickey, Pluto, etc., 4½" x 4½", made of material, by Pliotoys, Inc., USA.

Good | Excellent | Mint
$70 | **$100** | **$140**

Disney

Donald Duck Car, 6½", by Sun Rubber Co., USA.

Good	Excellent	Mint
$60	$100	$170

Mickey's Tractor, 4½", by Sun Rubber Co., USA.

Good	Excellent	Mint
$60	$100	$160

Mickey Mouse Air Mail, 6½", made in USA.

Good	Excellent	Mint
$65	$110	$170

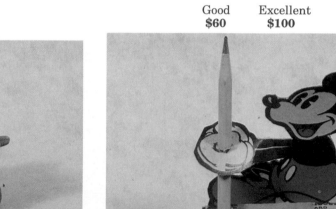

Mickey Mouse Pencil Holder, 3¼".

Good	Excellent	Mint
$5	$15	$25

1940 Pinocchio, 9", wind-up, by Marx, USA.

Good	Excellent	Mint
$485	$720	$1000

Horses, Cowboys, Circus etc

Zebra pulling Elephant,
9¼"long x 8½" high, wind-up.
Made in Germany.

Good	Excellent	Mint
$110	$175	$225

Mechanical Strutting Parade, Duck Cowboy Twirling Lariat, 8¼", wind-up, with original box. By Alps, Japan.

Good	Excellent	Mint
$120	$180	$200

Horse and Trainer, 9", by C.K. Japan.

Good	Excellent	Mint
$110	$200	$275

Horses, Cowboys, Circus etc

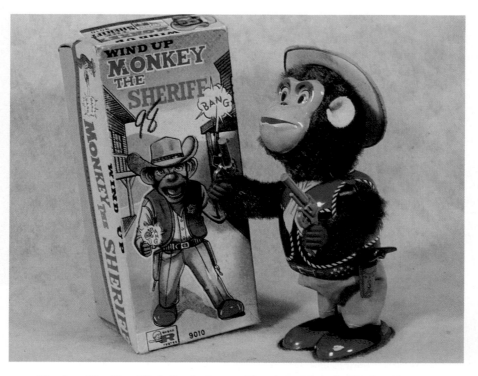

Monkey The Sheriff, 6¾", wind-up, with original box, by Rosko, Japan.

Good	Excellent	Mint
$80	**$120**	**$150**

Sheriff with Shooting Cork Gun, 7", with original box. By Yonezawa, Japan.

Good	Excellent	Mint
$80	**$110**	**$145**

Horses, Cowboys, Circus etc

Donkey, 5½", wind-up,
made in Japan.

Good	Excellent	Mint
$45	$70	$100

Soldier on his Horse, 5", wind-up,
made in Japan.

Good	Excellent	Mint
$40	$65	$90

Circus Wagon with Horses, 14",
by Kenton.

Good	Excellent	Mint
$300	$450	$600

Horses, Cowboys, Circus etc

Horse and Cart, 9", wind-up, by Marx, USA.

Good	Excellent	Mint
$100	$130	$160

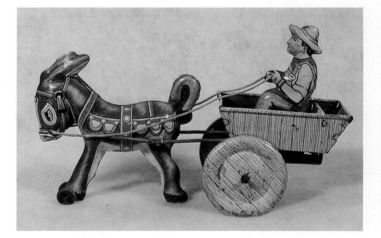

Donkey and Cart, 8½", wind-up, by Marx, USA.

Good	Excellent	Mint
$85	$100	$140

Lone Ranger Doll, 20"

Good	Excellent	Mint
$300	$450	$600

Horses, Cowboys, Circus etc

Cowboy, 9½", wind-up.

Good	Excellent	Mint
$40	**$100**	**$150**

Cow, press the tail and he Moo's,
tin, 10½".

Good	Excellent	Mint
$80	**$110**	**$150**

Motorcycles
Cast Iron

A.C. Williams Bike, 4¼".

Good	Excellent	Mint
$170	**$350**	**$550**

1. Motorcycle Cop, 4".
2. Motorcycle Cop Champion, 5".
3. Motorcycle Cop Champion, 5".
4. Motorcycle Cop, 4".

$150 to $225

Patrol Motorcycle, 6½".

Good	Excellent	Mint
$175	**$350**	**$500**

Champion Motorcycle, 7¼".

Good	Excellent	Mint
$200	**$350**	**$550**

Motorcycles
Cast Iron

Harley Davidson, 9", by Hubley.

Good	Excellent	Mint
$800	**$1200**	**$1500**

Motorcycle with side car, 8½",
battery operated headlight, by
Hubley.

Good	Excellent
$1400	**$1850**

Motorcycle, 9", by Hubley.

Good	Excellent
$450	**$700**

Motorcycles
Cast Iron

1930's Harley Davidsion, 5½",
by Hubley.

Good	Excellent	Mint
$200	**$275**	**$375**

1930's Harley Davidsion, 6",
by Hubley.

Good	Excellent	Mint
$325	**$400**	**$500**

Harley Davidson #45, Rider #2, 6½".

Good	Excellent
$290	**$550**

Harley Davidsion, 7¼".

Good	Excellent	Mint
$200	**$375**	**$500**

Harley Davidsion, 7¼".

Good	Excellent	Mint
$200	**$375**	**$500**

Motorcycles
Cast Iron

Flower Delivery Cycle, 4½".

Good	Excellent	Mint
$350	$600	$800

Indian Traffic Car, 8¾", by Hubley.

Good	Excellent	Mint
$900	$1800	$3550

German Motorcycles

Motorcycle, 7¾", wind-up, by Arnold, Germany.

Good	Excellent	Mint
$265	**$340**	**$440**

Mac 700 Black Motorcycle, 7½", wind-up, with original box. By Arnold, Germany.

Good	Excellent	Mint
$400	**$750**	**$900**

Mac 700 Red Motorcycle, 7½", wind-up, with original box. By Arnold, Germany.

Good	Excellent	Mint
$600	**$950**	**$1100**

German Motorcycles

Motorcycle Circus Act, 11½",
wind-up, with original box. By
Arnold, Germany.

Good   Excellent   Mint
$170 $235 $320

Monkey on 3 Wheeler, 3½", wind-up,
by D.R.G.M., Germany.

Good   Excellent   Mint
$160 $200 $240

Motodrill 1006, No. 5 & No. 2,
5", by Schuco, US Zone, Germany.

Good   Excellent   Mint
$225 $375 $500

German Motorcycles

Curvo 1000, 5", with original box, by Schuco, Germany.

Good	Excellent	Mint
$275	**$400**	**$500**

Motorcycle Racer, 7", wind-up, by Technofix, Germany.

Good	Excellent	Mint
$180	**$240**	**$300**

Motorcycle Racer, 7", wind-up, by Technofix, Germany.

Good	Excellent	Mint
$180	**$240**	**$300**

Double Rider Motorcycle, 6½", friction powered, by Technofix, Germany.

Good	Excellent	Mint
$200	**$275**	**$350**

Motorcycle Racer No. 15, 7¼", friction powered, by Technofix, Germany.

Good	Excellent	Mint
$100	**$145**	**$170**

German Motorcycles

Motorcycle Racer, 7", wind-up, by Technofix, Germany.

Good	Excellent	Mint
$110	**$200**	**$350**

Motorcycle with saddlebags, 7", by Tipp, Germany.

Good	Excellent	Mint
$700	**$1000**	**$1500**

Motorcycle with side car, 7¾", wind-up, by Tipp, Germany.

Good	Excellent	Mint
$750	**$1200**	**$1600**

Motorcycles with Soldiers, 4", made in Germany.

Good	Excellent	Mint
$300	**$420**	**$500**

German Motorcycles

Motorcycle with side car, 5", wind-up, made in Germany.

Good	Excellent	Mint
$200	**$250**	**$350**

Motorcycle, 3", made in Germany.

Good	Excellent	Mint
$75	**$180**	**$275**

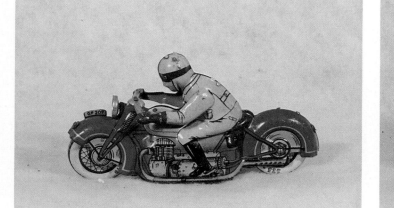

Motorcycle, 5¼", wind-up, made in Germany.

Good	Excellent	Mint
$150	**$220**	**$280**

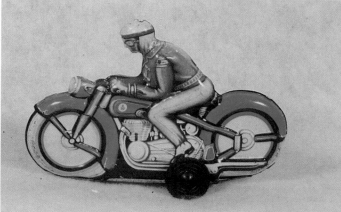

Motorcycle, 6½", made in Germany.

Good	Excellent	Mint
$100	**$160**	**$200**

Military Police Motorcycle with side car, 4", made in Germany.

Good	Excellent	Mint
$100	**$150**	**$250**

German Motorcycles

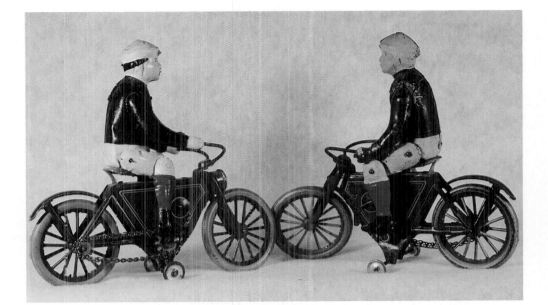

Motorcycles, 8", made in Germany.

Good	Excellent	Mint
$1000	**$1450**	**$1900**

Monkey on Tricycle, 4¾", made in Germany.

Good	Excellent	Mint
$650	**$800**	**$1000**

Police Figure 8 Motorcycle Twins, 6½", with original box. Made in West Germany.

Good	Excellent	Mint
$240	**$395**	**$490**

Japan Motorcycles

Police Auto Cycle, 11½", battery operated remote control, with original box. By Bandai, Japan.

Good	Excellent	Mint
$50	$70	$90

Speeding Car 7" and Motorcycle Policeman 3½", with original box. By FT, Japan.

Good	Excellent	Mint
$100	$175	$250

Motorcycle Trooper, 10", friction powered, by Hadson, Japan.

Good	Excellent	Mint
$400	$600	$750

Japan Motorcycles

Motorcycle Racer, 5¼", friction powered, by Hadson, Japan.

Good	Excellent	Mint
$60	**$90**	**$120**

Girl Cycle, 8", friction powered, with original box. By Haji, Japan.

Good	Excellent	Mint
$40	**$85**	**$125**

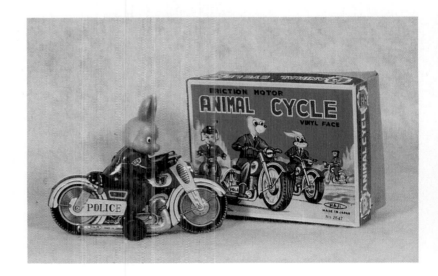

Animal Cycle Police, 5¼", with original box, by Haji, Japan.

Good	Excellent	Mint
$40	**$80**	**$100**

Japan Motorcycles

Motorcycle Racer, 5¼", friction powered, by Howa, Japan.

Good	Excellent	Mint
$140	**$180**	**$220**

Police Dept. Cycle, 6¼", mechanical, by KD, Japan.

Good	Excellent	Mint
$100	**$175**	**$220**

Monkey Rider, 6", wind-up, with original box. By Kanto Toys, Japan.

Good	Excellent	Mint
$225	**$350**	**$475**

Japan Motorcycles

Police Motorcycle, 7", by Line Mar
Toys, Japan.

Good	Excellent	Mint
$150	**$225**	**$350**

Highway Patrol Motorcycle, 11³/₄",
battery

Good	Excellent	Mint
$300	**$450**	**$600**

1950's Motorcycle, 11¹/₂", by
Modern Toys, Japan.

Good	Excellent	Mint
$200	**$400**	**$500**

Japan Motorcycles

Motorcycle Racer #25, 3¾",
by Stone, Japan.

Good	Excellent	Mint
$45	**$100**	**$150**

Daredevil Stunt Motorcyclist,
10¼", with original box. By TN, Japan.

Good	Excellent	Mint
$220	**$340**	**$400**

MP Motorcycle, 6", Indian,
friction powered, by TN, Japan.

Good	Excellent	Mint
$220	**$325**	**$560**

Japan Motorcycles

Harley Davidson Auto Cycle,
9", friction powered, with original
box. By TN, Japan.

Good	Excellent	Mint
$260	**$400**	**$495**

Venus Cycle, 9", friction powered,
by TN, Japan.

Good	Excellent	Mint
$240	**$380**	**$460**

Police Patrol Motorcycle, 8",
friction powered, with original
box. By TN, Japan.

Good	Excellent	Mint
$155	**$220**	**$325**

Japan Motorcycles

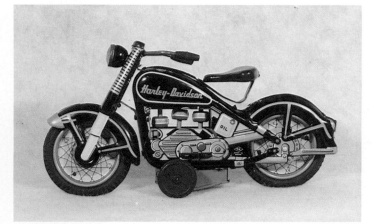

Harley Davidson Motorcycle, 9",
friction powered, by TN, Japan.

Good	Excellent	Mint
$250	**$390**	**$485**

Shooting Dispatch Rider, 61/2",
with original box. By Tydy, Japan.

Good	Excellent	Mint
$275	**$350**	**$450**

Harley Davidson Motorcycle No. 7 Racer, 5¼",
made in Japan.

Good	Excellent	Mint
$140	**$175**	**$250**

Clown on Motorcycle, 6¼", wind-up, made in Japan.

Good	Excellent	Mint
$250	**$350**	**$460**

Japan Motorcycles

1950's MP Motorcycle, 5¹/₄", made in Japan.

Good	Excellent	Mint
$140	**$275**	**$350**

Motorcycle, 5¹/₄", made in Japan.

Good	Excellent	Mint
$140	**$210**	**$270**

MP Motorcycle, 5¹/₄", made in Japan.

Good	Excellent	Mint
$110	**$145**	**$185**

Motorcycle Racer #1, 5", wind-up, made in Japan.

Good	Excellent	Mint
$140	**$180**	**$220**

PD Motorcycle, 4³/₄", wind-up, made in Japan.

Good	Excellent	Mint
$100	**$120**	**$150**

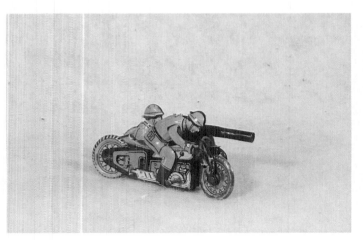

Military Police Motorcycle with gun, 4", made in Japan.

Good	Excellent	Mint
$100	**$150**	**$200**

Japan Motorcycles

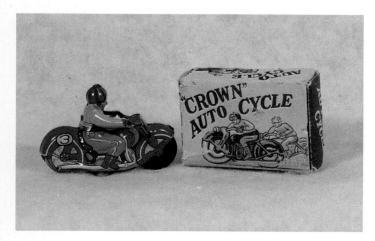

1950's Crown Auto Cycle No. 3, 3½",
with original box. Made in Japan.

Good	Excellent	Mint
$45	$75	$100

Racing Motorcycle No. 18, 3½",
made in Japan.

Good	Excellent	Mint
$25	$30	$50

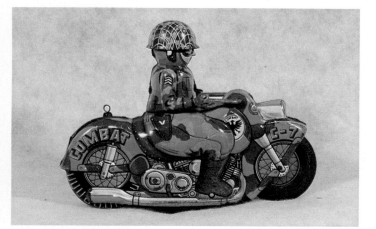

Motorcycle Combat, 8", made in Japan.

Good	Excellent	Mint
$120	$200	$245

US Motorcycles

Police Motorcycle, 4¼", friction powered, by Marx, USA.

Good	Excellent	Mint
$90	$120	$140

Police Motorcycle with side car, 8¼", by Marx, USA.

Good	Excellent	Mint
$130	$185	$275

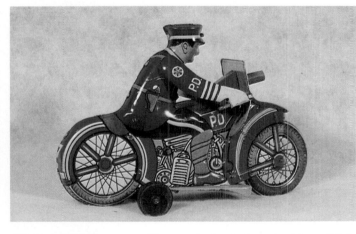

Motorcycle Policeman with gun, 8½", wind-up, by Marx, USA.

Good	Excellent	Mint
$175	$330	$400

Police Motorcycle, 8¾", by Marx, USA.

Good	Excellent	Mint
$240	$290	$350

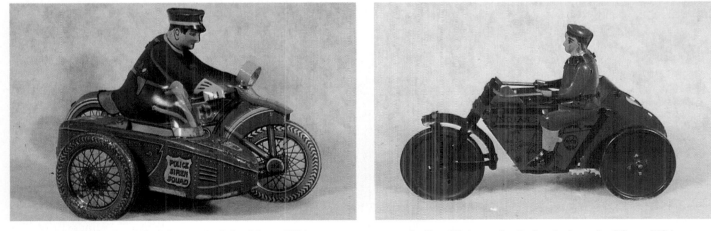

Police Cycle with side car, 8¼", by Marx, USA.

Good	Excellent	Mint
$150	$270	$350

Indian Motorcycle, 6¼", wind-up, by Marx, USA.

Good	Excellent	Mint
$425	$670	$800

US Motorcycles

Three Wheel Police Motorcycle, 4",
by Marx.

Good	Excellent	Mint
$175	**$250**	**$375**

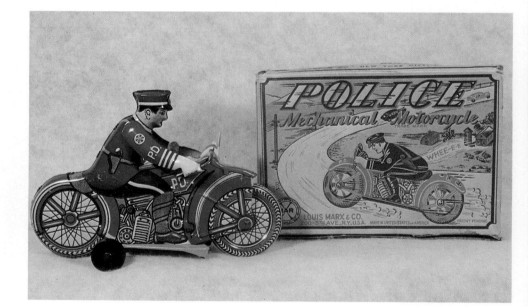

Police Siren Motorcycle, 8½",
wind-up, with original box. By
Marx, USA.

Good	Excellent	Mint
$200	**$250**	**$300**

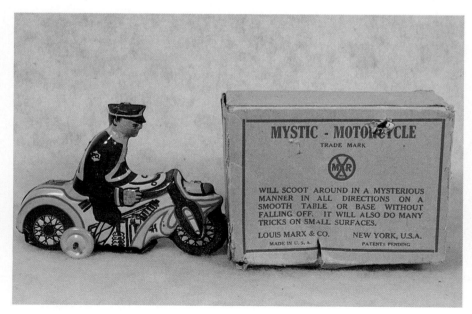

Mystic Motorcycle, 4¼", wind-up,
by Marx, USA.

Good	Excellent	Mint
$80	**$130**	**$160**

US Motorcycles

Motorcycle No. 3, 8½", wind-up, by Marx, USA.

Good	Excellent	Mint
$110	**$160**	**$245**

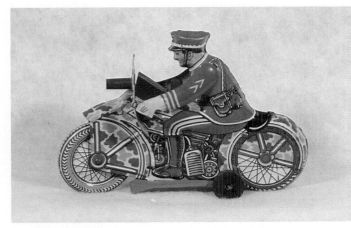

Motorcycle with gun, 8½", wind-up, by Marx, USA.

Good	Excellent	Mint
$195	**$350**	**$425**

Motorcycle plastic whistle, 4⅛".

Good	Excellent	Mint
$20	**$30**	**$45**

Delivery Cycle, 9¾", by Nylint, Rockford, IL.

Good	Excellent	Mint
$100	**$185**	**$260**

Miscellaneous Motorcycles

Motorcycle, 6½", wind-up, by RSA, Rico Spain.

Good	Excellent	Mint
$160	**$200**	**$250**

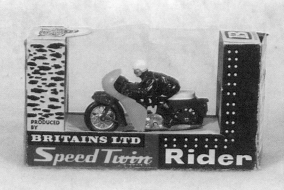

Britains Ltd. Speed Twin Rider, 2½", with original box, made in England.

Good	Excellent	Mint
$20	**$30**	**$45**

1932 Auto Cycle, Les Jouets, 9½", French.

Good	Excellent	Mint
$600	**$800**	**$1100**

Motorcycle, 6", with side car.

Good	Excellent	Mint
$210	**$265**	**$350**

Motorcycle, 3½", diecast.

Good	Excellent	Mint
$20	**$30**	**$40**

Penny Toys

Animals on wheels, approx. 3",
made in Germany.

Good	Excellent	Mint
$95	$125	$185

Horse pulling cart, 4½'.

Good	Excellent	Mint
$100	$165	$200

Donkey pulling cart, 4½".

Good	Excellent	Mint
$90	$130	$165

Car No. 8, 4½".

Good	Excellent	Mint
$140	$175	$225

Mobile Gas Station, 4".

Good	Excellent	Mint
$90	$150	$200

Penny Toys

Racers, sizes: 4", 3¼", 4", 4¾".
Made in Germany.

$150 to $500

Campsa Truck Tanker, 4¼".

Good	Excellent	Mint
$100	**$155**	**$190**

Automobile with passengers, 4½".

Good	Excellent	Mint
$175	**$260**	**$400**

Carriage, 3" long.

Good	Excellent	Mint
$120	**$180**	**$230**

Automobile, 3½" long, made in Germany.

Good	Excellent	Mint
$110	**$150**	**$175**

Penny Toys

First Aid Wagon, 3¼", made in Germany.

Good	Excellent	Mint
$200	**$275**	**$375**

Convertible Automobile, 4", made in Germany.

Good	Excellent	Mint
$90	**$180**	**$240**

Automobile, 2¾", made in Germany.

Good	Excellent	Mint
$110	**$150**	**$175**

Penny Toy, 2½".

Good	Excellent	Mint
$70	**$125**	**$175**

Train, 5½" long.

Good	Excellent	Mint
$80	**$140**	**$175**

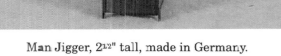

Man Jigger, 2½" tall, made in Germany.

Good	Excellent	Mint
$350	**$450**	**$550**

Penny Toys

Penny Toys on the ends of whistles, made in Germany.

$150 to $550

Penny Toy, 2¹⁄₂".

Good	Excellent	Mint
$65	**$85**	**$110**

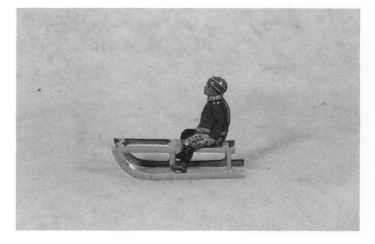

Boy on a Sled, 2¹⁄₂", made in Germany.

Good	Excellent	Mint
$120	**$180**	**$250**

Kid's in Highchairs, 2³⁄₄" and 4", made in Germany.

Good	Excellent	Mint
$160	**$250**	**$325**

Baby Carriage, 3³⁄₄".

Good	Excellent	Mint
$80	**$110**	**$160**

Spaceships

Space Patrol Z-206, 7³⁄₄", battery operated, by TPS, Japan.

Good	Excellent	Mint
$140	**$200**	**$240**

Atomic Spaceship, 12³⁄₄", friction powered, with original box. By TN, Japan.

Good	Excellent	Mint
$80	**$100**	**$150**

Rocket Spaceship, 9", with original box. By Automatic Toy Co., USA.

Good	Excellent	Mint
$100	**$200**	**$300**

Spaceships

Tom Corbett Sparkling Space Cadet
Ship, 12", with original box, wind-up.
By Marx, USA.

Good	Excellent	Mint
$400	$600	$800

Rocket Fighter, 12½", by Louis
Marx.

Good	Excellent	Mint
$300	$400	$490

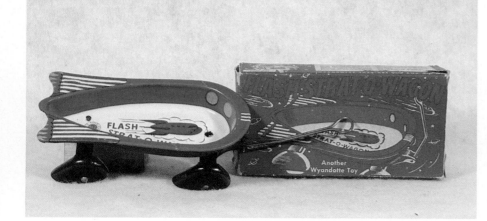

Strat-o-Wagon, 6", with original box.
By Wyandotte, USA.

Good	Excellent	Mint
$70	$90	$120

Tootsietoys

Rocket Launching Set (two views: front of box and inside of box)
17³/₄" x 13¹/₂".

Good	Excellent	Mint
$225	**$300**	**$375**

Tootsietoys

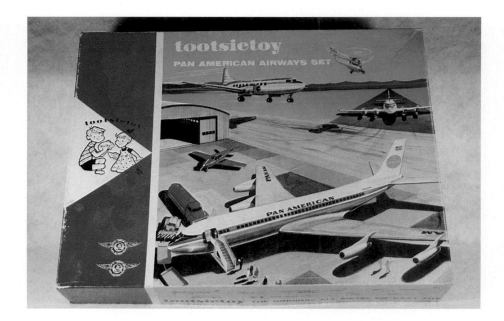

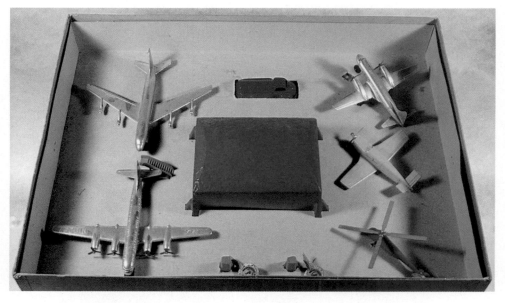

Pan American Airways Set, (two views: front of box and inside of box)
17³/⁴" x 13¹/²".

Good	Excellent	Mint
$250	**$350**	**$400**

Tootsietoys

Motorcycle Delivery, 3".

Good | Excellent | Mint
$180 | $350 | $450

Logger Truck, 9" long, with original box.

Good | Excellent | Mint
$45 | S80 | $100

Oil Tanker, 9" long, with original box.

Good | Excellent | Mint
$50 | $90 | $110

Tootsietoys

Van Semi with removable top,
9" long, with original box.

Good	Excellent	Mint
$45	**$80**	**$100**

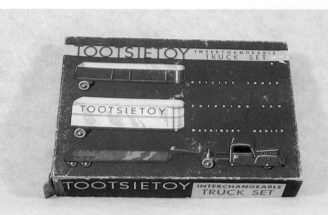

Interchangeable Truck Set, 8" x 11½",
with original box.

Set – **$250**

Left:
Interchangeable Truck Set,
with original box.

Good	Excellent	Mint
$100	**$140**	**$175**

Right:
Trailer Truck Set, with original
box.

Good	Excellent	Mint
$120	**$170**	**$200**

Tootsietoys

Milk Trailers, 13¼", with original box.

Good	Excellent	Mint
$150	**$200**	**$260**

Trucks, 2½", 3", and 3".

Good	Excellent	Mint
$55	**$100**	**$135**

Auto Transport, 9" long, with original box.

Good	Excellent	Mint
$75	**$95**	**$120**

Auto Transport 9½" long, with original box.

Good	Excellent	Mint
$80	**$100**	**$130**

Tootsietoys

Auto Transport, 10¾", with original box.

Good	Excellent	Mint
$150	**$200**	**$250**

Playtime Miniatures No. 7005, with original box.

Set with box – **$850**

Farm Tractor Set. No. 7003, Playtime Miniatures, with original box.

Set with box – **$900**

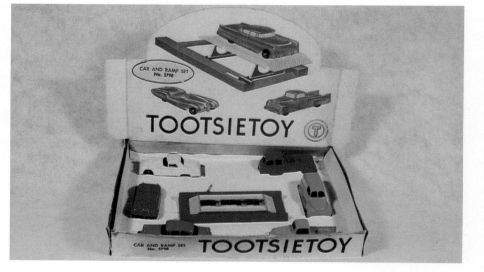

Car and Ramp set No. 5798, 10½", with original box.

Set with box – **$250**

Scooters and Bikes

Tricycle/Go-Cart, tin and celluloid, 5", wind-up, made in Japan.

Good	Excellent	Mint
$220	**$300**	**$380**

Prewar Baby Car, tin and celluloid, 6¼",
made in Tokyo, Japan.

Good	Excellent	Mint
$250	**$310**	**$390**

Dog and Bicycle, 5½", wind-up, made in Japan.

Good	Excellent	Mint
$95	**$150**	**$175**

Prewar Delivery Cycle, 7¼", wind-up, made in Japan.

Good	Excellent	Mint
$900	**$1400**	**$1800**

Prewar Bike with Rider, tin and
celluloid, 5", wind-up, with original
box. Made in Japan.

Good	Excellent	Mint
$100	**$165**	**$225**

Scooters and Bikes

1950's Patrol Auto-Tricycle, battery operated. By Nomura, Japan.

Good	Excellent	Mint
$110	$225	$300

Vespa Scooter G.S., 8¾",
friction powered, by Bandai,
Japan.

Good	Excellent	Mint
$170	$290	$340

Animal Scooter, 3½", wind-up,
with original box. By Haji, Japan.

Good	Excellent	Mint
$50	$70	$90

Scooters and Bikes

Circus Tricycle, 5", Occupied
Japan. By LW & Co., Japan.

Good	Excellent	Mint
$40	$75	$100

Tricycle Scooter, 3¾", Occupied
Japan, wind-up.

Good	Excellent	Mint
$40	$75	$100

Monkey Tricycle, 2¾", tin and celluloid,
made in Japan.

Good	Excellent	Mint
$35	$100	$125

Tiger on a Tricycle, 3¾", wind-up,
by Marx Toys, Japan.

Good	Excellent	Mint
$55	$110	$175

Scooters and Bikes

Tricycle Tot Scooter, 4½" x 4½", wind-up, with original box. By TPS, Japan.

Good	Excellent	Mint
$90	$120	$160

Duck on a Tricycle, 4½", made in Japan.

Good	Excellent	Mint
$175	$270	$350

Boy on a Scooter (Flyer), 8½", by B & R, USA.

Good	Excellent	Mint
$235	$400	$500

Miscellaneous Toys

Football Kicker, 8", cast iron,
made in USA.

Good	Excellent	Mint
$100	**$150**	**$190**

Reading Santa Claus, 7",
by Alps, Japan.

Good	Excellent	Mint
$50	**$90**	**$125**

Boy on Ski's, 8", wind-up,
by J. Chein, USA.

Good	Excellent	Mint
$100	**$145**	**$185**

Miscellaneous Toys

Salesman, 8½", wind-up, by
Martn France

Good	Excellent	Mint
$600	**$800**	**$1000**

Skating Chef, 6½", wind-up,
by TPS, Japan.

Good	Excellent	Mint
$100	**$165**	**$200**

Violin Player, 5½", wind-up,
by Line Mar, Japan.

Good	Excellent	Mint
$130	**$200**	**$260**

Miscellaneous Toys

Trumpet Player, 9½", wind-up,
with original box. Made in
Japan.

Good	Excellent	Mint
$165	**$225**	**$290**

Police Man, 5½", by Chein, USA.

Good	Excellent	Mint
$50	**$85**	**$120**

Prewar Drummer, 6" tall,
wind-up, made in Japan.

Good	Excellent	Mint
$110	**$170**	**$200**

Miscellaneous Toys

Marching Drummer, 6" tall,
wind-up, by Line Mar, Japan.

Good	Excellent	Mint
$120	**$180**	**$225**

Drummer, 13" tall, wind-up,
made in USA.

Good	Excellent	Mint
$75	**$110**	**$160**

Advertising Bank for Dodge,
4" high.

Good	Excellent	Mint
$30	**$45**	**$65**

Miscellaneous Toys

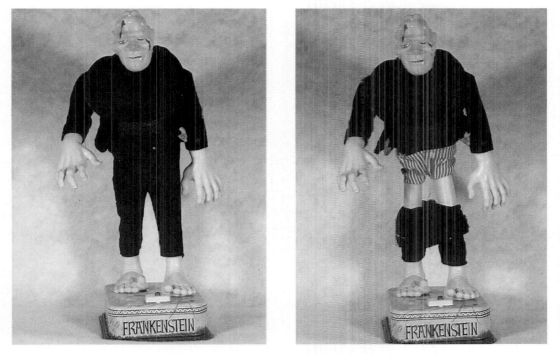

Frankenstein, 13½", battery operated.

Good	Excellent	Mint
$75	$110	$175

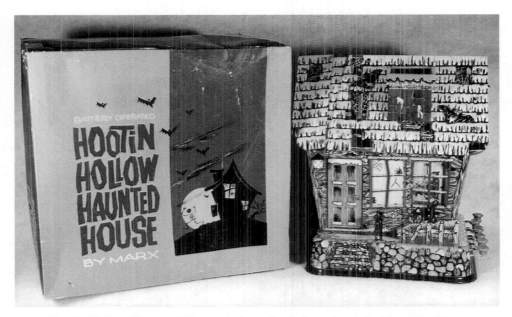

Hootin Hollow Haunted House, 8¾" x 11" x 7½", with original box. By Marx.

Good	Excellent	Mint
$600	$750	$900

Miscellaneous Toys

Ol' Sleepy Head Rip, 9½" x 5",
with original box. By Spesco, Japan.

Good	Excellent	Mint
$90	$120	$160

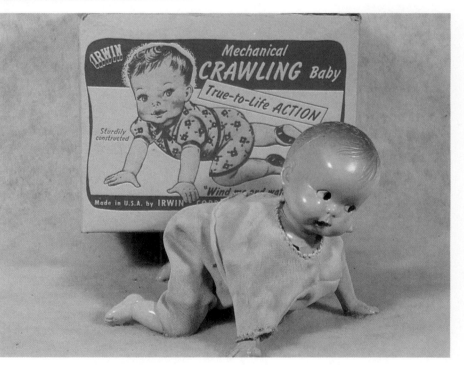

Crawling Baby, 5¼" long, wind-up,
with original box. By Irwin, USA.

Good	Excellent	Mint
$45	$70	$90

Nina Mother's Helper, 9" x 8", with
original box. By Irwin Co., USA.

Set with box – **$150**

Miscellaneous Toys

Crawling Baby, 4¼" long, wind-up, with original box. Made in Japan.

Good	Excellent	Mint
$40	**$65**	**$80**

Baby in a Bed, 5" long, with original box. Made in Hong Kong.

Good	Excellent	Mint
S15	**$25**	**$35**

Child Indian, 6¾", wind-up, made in Japan.

Good	Excellent	Mint
$80	**$120**	**$145**

Miscellaneous Toys

Monkey balancing on chairs, 4" wide,
wind-up, made in Japan.

Good	Excellent	Mint
$65	**$110**	**$160**

Monkey Drummer, 4¹/²" tall,
wind-up, by Schuco, Germany.

Good	Excellent	Mint
$70	**$130**	**$150**

Bear Painting, 6³/⁴", wind-up,
made in Japan.

Good	Excellent	Mint
$50	**$100**	**$125**

Miscellaneous Toys

Monkey Batter, 6½", wind-up, with original box. By AAA, Japan.

Good	Excellent	Mint
$160	**$200**	**$285**

Greeting Monkey, 5¾", wind-up, with original box, by SY, Japan.

Good	Excellent	Mint
$60	**$80**	**$100**

Bombo, 6" x 9½", by Unique Art Mfg. Co., Newark, N.J.

Good	Excellent	Mint
$80	**$150**	**$175**

Miscellaneous Toys

Table Monkey Playing Pool, 4¼",
wind-up, by TPS, Japan.

Good	Excellent	Mint
$75	**$100**	**$125**

Rock'nRoll Monkey, 11" tall, battery
operated, with original box. Made in
Japan.

Good	Excellent	Mint
$90	**$110**	**$145**

Cat (push tail to wind), 8½",
by Marx.

Good	Excellent	Mint
$50	**$80**	**$120**

Miscellaneous Toys

Tricky Tommy Dog, 6¼", wind-up,
with original box. By Marx Toys, Japan.

Good	Excellent	Mint
$20	$40	$65

Jumbo Elephant, 4¼", wind-up,
made in Germany.

Good	Excellent	Mint
$80	$110	$150

Elephant, tin, friction powered, 9".

Good	Excellent	Mint
$100	$200	$300

Miscellaneous Toys

Bear Playing Cymbals, 6½", wind-up,
made in Japan.

Good	Excellent	Mint
$50	**$80**	**$100**

Bear Drinking Milk, 5¼", wind-up,
made in Japan.

Good	Excellent	Mint
$60	**$100**	**$125**

Miscellaneous Toys

Chicken, 9½", battery operated, by Marx, Japan.

Good	Excellent	Mint
$60	**$90**	**$125**

Rabbit playing Accordian, 6¾", wind-up, made in Japan.

Good	Excellent	Mint
$50	**$85**	**$110**

Cubby The Reading Bear, 7", wind-up, with original box. Made in Japan.

Good	Excellent	Mint
$80	**$100**	**$125**

Miscellaneous Toys

Bear riding Donkey, 4½", wind-up, made in Japan.

Good	Excellent	Mint
$40	$80	$100

Bear Knitting, 6½", wind-up, made in Japan.

Good	Excellent	Mint
$60	$80	$100

Bear Ironing, 6", wind-up, made in Japan.

Good	Excellent	Mint
$80	$100	$120

Golfing Bear, 4" tall, by TPS, Japan.

Good	Excellent	Mint
$70	$90	$130

Miscellaneous Toys

Bear Drinking Coffee, 11",
battery operated, made in Japan.

Good	Excellent	Mint
$30	$70	$90

Bear Peanut Vendor, 9½", battery
operated, by TN, Japan.

Good	Excellent	Mint
$160	$210	$260

Dancing Cat (Puss & Boots), 5",
by Gesch, Germany.

Good	Excellent	Mint
$85	$120	$150

Miscellaneous Toys

Bunny on Skis, 4½", wind-up.

Good	Excellent	Mint
$70	**$100**	**$130**

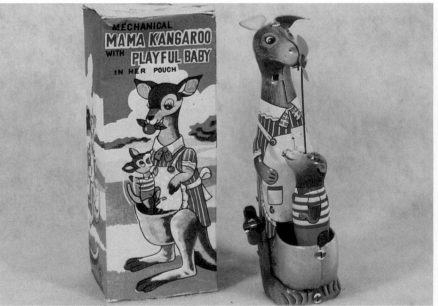

Mama Kangaroo with Playful Baby,
6" high, wind-up, with original box.
By TPB, Japan.

Good	Excellent	Mint
$90	**$135**	**$160**

Candy Loving Canine, 5½", wind-up,
by TPS, Japan.

Good	Excellent	Mint
$65	**$110**	**$150**

Miscellaneous Toys

Jumpin Jeep, 5½", wind-up, by Marx, USA.

Good	Excellent	Mint
$80	$110	S160

Cowboy Crazy Car, 7½", wind-up, with original box, by Unique Art Mfg. Co., USA.

Good	Excellent	Mint
$175	$270	$390

G.I. Joe Crazy Car Jeep, 6½", wind-up, by Unique Art Mfg. Co., USA.

Good	Excellent	Mint
$165	$220	$275

Highboy Climbing Tractor, 10", by Marx, USA.

Good	Excellent	Mint
$90	$120	$165

Miscellaneous Toys

Caterpillar, 5¹/₂", by Arcade.

Good	Excellent	Mint
$300	**$400**	**$600**

Caterpillar, 6³/₄", with original box, by Arcade.

Good	Excellent	Mint
$450	**$900**	**$1200**

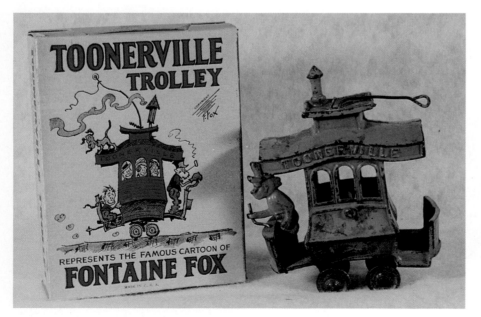

Toonerville Trolley, 4¹/₄", cast iron, with original box, by Dent.

Good	Excellent	Mint
$450	**$600**	**$900**

Miscellaneous Toys

Matador with Bull, 9", wind-up,
made in Germany.

Good	Excellent	Mint
$300	**$500**	**$600**

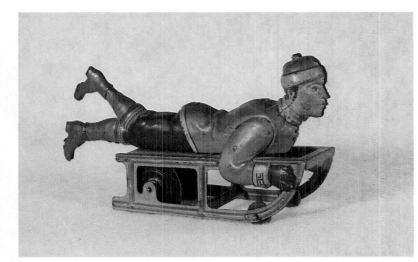

Boy on Sled, 6¼", by Hess, Germany.

Good	Excellent	Mint
$300	**$400**	**$550**

Kid's Special, 6¼", by B & R.

Good	Excellent	Mint
$250	**$385**	**$475**

Miscellaneous Toys

Man in Car, 8", wind-up, by Marx, USA.

Good	Excellent	Mint
$250	**$400**	**$525**

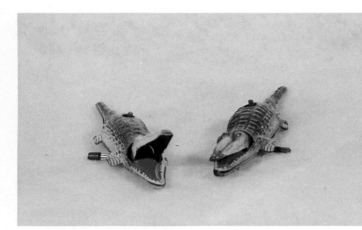

Alligator, 5¼", wind-up, tin.

Good	Excellent	Mint
$30	**$45**	**$65**

Alligator, 8", pull toy, made in Germany.

Good	Excellent	Mint
$140	**$190**	**$240**

Hone-In-One Bank, 8½", battery operated, with original box, made in Japan.

Good	Excellent	Mint
$45	**$90**	**$125**

Miscellaneous Toys

Commando Joe, 8", wind-up, by Ohio Art, USA.

Good	Excellent	Mint
$75	**$90**	**$110**

Crawling Indian, 8½" long, by Ohio Art Co., Bryan, Ohio.

Good	Excellent	Mint
$65	**$90**	**$120**

Combat Tank with Recoiling Cannon, 9", with original box, by Marx.

Good	Excellent	Mint
$65	**$100**	**$130**

Miscellaneous Toys

Juke Box Bank, 4¹/₂" x 3³/₄", wind-up music, by Haji, Japan.

Good	Excellent	Mint
$110	**$155**	**$190**

Mechanical Billiard Table, 14¹/₄", by Ranger Steel Products Co., USA.

Good	Excellent	Mint
$150	**$185**	**$225**

Carnival Ride, 13" x 15", battery operated remote, by Alps, Japan.

Good	Excellent	Mint
$400	**$575**	**$750**

Miscellaneous Toys

Miss Busy-Bee The Typist, 3½" x 5¼",
with original box, by Kanto Toys, Japan.

Good	Excellent	Mint
$60	$100	$140

Miss Friday The Typist, 8",
with original box. Made in Japan.

Good	Excellent	Mint
$50	$90	$175

Dolly Seamstress, 5", battery
operated, with original box, by
TN, Japan.

Good	Excellent	Mint
$90	$120	$150

Miscellaneous Toys

Jaeger Cement Mixer, 7½", cast iron, by Kenton.

Good	Excellent	Mint
$300	$700	$1000

Fairbanks Morse, 4", cast iron.

Good	Excellent	Mint
$110	$200	$350

Buck Rogers Disintegrator, 9½", by Daisy Mfg. Co.

Good	Excellent	Mint
$60	$90	$130

Buick Advertising Trash Cans, 3¾" tall and 2" wide.

Good	Excellent	Mint
$100	$140	$175

Miscellaneous Toys

Ranger Basketball, 6½" x 14", mechanical, by Ranger Steel Products, USA.

Good	Excellent	Mint
$70	$100	$140

Bing Phonograph, 6½", made in Germany.

Good	Excellent	Mint
$100	$150	$190

Man on the Flying Trapeze, 9", wind-up, with original box. By Wyandotte Toys, USA.

Good	Excellent	Mint
$110	$140	$170

Miscellaneous Toys

Washing Machine, 5¼", cast iron, by Arcase, USA.

Good	Excellent	Mint
$120	$220	$300

Maytag Washer, 7¼", cast iron.

Good	Excellent	Mint
$300	$575	$750

Mangle, 4¼", cast iron, by Arcade, USA.

Good	Excellent	Mint
$85	$100	$150

Miscellaneous Toys

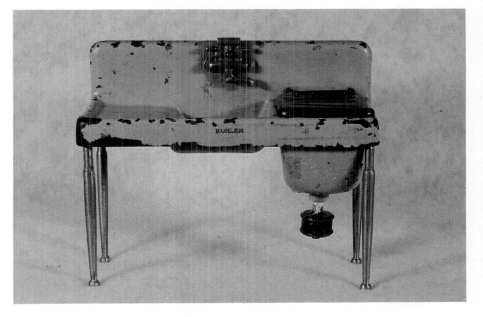

Sink, 6", cast iron, by Arcade, USA.

Good	Excellent	Mint
$65	$100	$150

Cream Separator, 5" high, by Arcade, USA.

Good	Excellent	Mint
$300	$500	$700

Marklin Bathroom around the 1900's, 14".

Good	Excellent	Mint
$2200	$3000	$6000